BE A MASTER
OF THE GAME

...that's taking the country by storm. From college dormitories to executive suites, everybody's playing Trivial Pursuit™—but with this one-and-only guidebook, you can learn to beat the best of them. Based on a winning combination of good moves, playing the averages, and most challenging of all, outthinking the gamemakers *and* your opponents, this exclusive approach turns a game of trivial knowledge into a game of real skill. Now all you need to become a winning player is—

WINNING AT
TRIVIAL
PURSUIT™

JEFF ROVIN, a Trivial Pursuit™ fanatic, is the creator of *Games* Magazine and is about to release a new magazine called *Trivia!* He is also the author of many books, including THE SIGNET BOOK OF TV LISTS and the soon-to-be-published TV BABYLON.

Ⓢ

Other SIGNET Books You'll Enjoy

WINNING AT TRIVIAL PURSUIT™

by
Jeff Rovin
Editor of *TRIVIA!* Magazine

A SIGNET BOOK

NEW AMERICAN LIBRARY

SIGNET TRADEMARK REG. U.S. PAT. OFF. AND FOREIGN COUNTRIES
REGISTERED TRADEMARK—MARCA REGISTRADA
HECHO EN CHICAGO, U.S.A.

SIGNET, SIGNET CLASSIC, MENTOR, PLUME, MERIDIAN
and NAL BOOKS are published by New American Library,
1633 Broadway, New York, New York 10019.

First Printing, June, 1984

1 2 3 4 5 6 7 8 9

PRINTED IN THE UNITED STATES OF AMERICA

ACKNOWLEDGMENTS

Jim and Liz Trupin, John Barylick, Steve Burkow, and Vincent and Rosanne DiFate; Claudia Reilly, Arnold Dolin, and the staff at NAL; and Samuel Rovin.

Contents

Part Six:
TRIVIA TOURNAMENTS 125

Part Seven:
EVERYTHING YOU EVER WANTED TO KNOW ABOUT THE OTHER TRIVIA GAMES ON THE MARKET 135

Part Eight:
WRITING AND SELLING NEW TRIVIA QUESTIONS FOR TRIVIAL PURSUIT™ 149

Part Nine:
ALL-NEW TRIVIA QUESTIONS TO HELP YOU GET STARTED WRITING YOUR OWN 171

Part Ten:
ALL-NEW CHILDREN'S QUESTIONS
TO HELP YOU GET STARTED WRITING
YOUR OWN 231

Introduction

It's been decades since a board game has become an instant classic. Monopoly™ did it; so did Scrabble™. Now Trivial Pursuit™ has joined their rarefied company, and before many months are out it may well establish itself as the most popular of them all.

Released in 1981, Trivial Pursuit requires players to move around a circular track, collecting wedges by answering trivia questions. These questions, printed on game cards, are in areas ranging from science to football to TV shows.

The success of Trivial Pursuit is such that in addition to the 6,000 questions which came with the original game, card sets containing an additional 18,000 questions have since been published.

Why has the game taken such a firm hold of our imagination? What does Trivial Pursuit have that other trivial media and traditional board games lack?

On the offensive, Trivial Pursuit allows us to ask our friends and families to reveal their knowledge—or lack of it. We can sit back and smile as others squirm. After all, *we* know the answers, and this makes us momentarily omnipotent—a feeling we have all too infrequently. It can be highly rewarding to revel in the suffering, oaths, and physical contortions of ignorant friends and family members who beg for the mercy of an answer.

On the defensive, racking our own brains to solve questions posed by some *other* smart aleck can be sweet pain. Trivia is actually aerobics for the mind—the intensity of concentration we muster up gets our brain moving in high gear. Trying to think of an answer can be harrowing, but once we've hit upon a correct response, we feel euphoric.

Obviously, the enjoyment of Trivial Pursuit depends in large part upon a sense of discovery. Players never know whether the next roll of the die is going to saddle them with a question about something easy (such as Simple Simon's destination when he met the pieman) or something murderous (such as the name of a girl in a 1950s song that even the composer's mother has surely forgotten). Hence, a book about how to win at Trivial Pursuit might seem, at first glance, to undermine the mystery of the game.

But mastering Trivial Pursuit involves far more than simply answering questions. Indeed, the better you understand the board, the cards, and what's going on inside your opponent's head, the more exciting play becomes—and the more often you'll win.

HOW THIS BOOK CAN HELP YOU WIN AT TRIVIAL PURSUIT™

Learn board strategies. Because Trivial Pursuit is a carefully constructed board game, there are various strategies for getting around it. Being aware of these tactics enhances rather than diminishes play.

Find your strongest categories. It's more fun watching your opponent shrug at you with a blank face than getting the fuzzy side of the lollipop yourself. Accordingly, if you elect to take a sports question, you should know what your chances are of getting a query about baseball as opposed to tiddlywinks.

Discover which answers on the cards are wrong. Though game makers try to be perfect, errors *do* slip into their work. You may very well save yourself a lost turn or fistfight by knowing that an answer *you* gave is correct and the one on the card is in error.

Learn how to spot trick questions and clued questions. There are many questions that help or mislead you by the way they are worded. You will want to know how to distinguish the bona fide clues from the booby traps.

Gain a psychological edge over opponents. As in poker, chess, and other games, psychology can be an effective tool. How you read a question and how you react—or don't react—to your opponent's musings can have dramatic consequences on the game.

Discover new games and new rules. The rules for Trivial Pursuit are surprisingly skimpy. For example, no time limits are set for a turn, and no guidelines are suggested regarding how accurately questions should be answered, what to do if an overzealous player accidentally hints at the answer, or how to handle a disputed answer. This book addresses those problems. It also provides play variations, including methods of handicapping advanced trivialists.

Find out which card sets and competitor's games are the best. There are strictly economic reasons for a book such as this. Trivial Pursuit and the other trivia games presently on the market are *expensive* pursuits. The basic game costs an average of $40, and additional card sets are $20 and up. The *Time* magazine game™ tips the fiscal scales at somewhat less than that, though it can rarely be had for under $19.95. Before you invest that kind of money, you have a right to sample what you're going to get: what kinds of topics and questions are contained, the nature of play, whether one game or card set is as good as another, and so forth.

Write your own questions. You and your fellow trivialists may be so trivia-hungry that not only do you buy everything and anything that comes out on the market, but you want to write your own. This book will tell you how to do so for fun and profit. *Winning at Trivial Pursuit* also contains hundreds of new questions and answers to assist you in creating new questions. There are, as well, 300 questions for children. As you'll discover, one of the satisfactions of writing your own questions is that you can have fun with all the latest headlines, fads, and superstars while they're still hot!

THE HISTORY OF TRIVIA

Winning at Trivial Pursuit performs one other very necessary public service. Despite having secured a place as one of the preeminent games of our generation, Trivial Pursuit and trivia in general are occasionally mocked by snooty and elitist writers, commentators, and next-door neighbors. For handy reference, herewith is evidence that we trivia buffs have the weight of history and scholarship on our side!

For example, in his treatise *De finibus*, the great Roman lawyer and orator Cicero stated that anyone not possessing some trivial knowledge suffers from "a refinement of taste carried to the point of caprice." A few centuries later, the distinguished English statesman Edmund Burke said that among his peers, "the wisest in council, the ablest in debate, and the most agreeable in the commerce of life, is that man who has assimilated to his understanding the greatest number of facts." We can also infer from his works that Shakespeare was a trivia booster; why else would he have scattered throughout his plays the likes of the unrenowned fruit *medlar*, the un-revered Tartar khan *Cham*, and the even then unpopular game of *span-counter*? Abraham Lincoln, too, was an avid trivialist, having once declared that people shouldn't be happy until they'd learned everything they could about a subject by following it "to the north, south, east, and west."

Shakespeare, Lincoln, Cicero—august company indeed. Yet, perhaps the most eloquent defense of trivia was made several years ago by the Monty Python comedy troupe. In a skit entitled "World Forum," a panel consisting of Chairman Mao, Lenin, Karl Marx, and Che Guevara was interviewed—about sports trivia. The dignitaries were befuddled and embarrassed, proving that the importance of knowledge is relative, determined solely by what someone else happens to want to know at the moment.

Thus, while the word "trivia" may derive from the Latin *trivialis* or "belonging to the crossroads"—in other words, that which is common to all and, hence, insignificant—there is nothing insignificant about trivia. Or about fun. Or about learning. And there's nothing insignificant about camaraderie. Trivia, and especially Trivial Pursuit, provide all these in abundance.

This book was designed to help you tap your trivia resources to the fullest. Consider *Winning at Trivial Pursuit* as the mental equivalent to *The Joy of Sex*: whatever equipment you bring to the game, you're going to learn how to use it a lot better.

Happy trivializing!

PART ONE

THE GAME OF
TRIVIAL PURSUIT™

How to Play
Trivial Pursuit™

The Genus Edition of Trivial Pursuit comes equipped with a board, two boxes of playing cards, a die, three dozen colored wedges, and six tokens. The object of the game is to be the first to fill one's token with wedges and then answer one final question. To accomplish this, a player moves around the "wheel" or up and down the "spokes" on the board by rolling a die and answering trivia questions in six different categories. A wedge is earned by landing on one of the six "headquarters" spaces on the wheel—there is one such space for each category—and correctly answering a question pertaining to that category. After earning all six wedges, a player moves along a spoke of the wheel to the wheel's "hub"—or center. There the player is asked a trivia question in whatever category his or her opponents select—usually, of course, in the one they consider the player's weakest. If the question is answered correctly, the game is over. If not, the player must keep playing, moving out of the hub and then trying to get back to the hub for another chance at a final question.

Including the six headquarters spaces, there are seventy-two spaces on the board. If you land on a space that is not a headquarters, you still must answer a question in the category the color indicates, or, in the case of a gray-colored space, roll again.

- If you land on a brown space, you must answer an Art & Literature question.
- If you land on a green space, you must answer a Science & Nature question.

- If you land on an orange space, you must answer a Sports & Leisure question.
- If you land on a pink space, you must answer an Entertainment question.
- If you land on a blue space, you must answer a Geography question.
- If you land on a yellow space, you must answer a History question.

Players may move their tokens forward or backward. They can move around the rim of the wheel or up and down the spokes. If they choose to move across the spokes of the wheel and land on the hub or center, they may pick their category.

When a player correctly answers a question, the player continues rolling the die and moving around the board until he or she answers a question incorrectly. At that point, the next player rolls and moves.

New Editions of Trivial Pursuit™

In addition to the Genus Edition—which is the only edition of Trivial Pursuit that comes equipped with game board, tokens, wedges, and die—there are three other editions of the game: Baby Boomer, Silver Screen, and All-Star Sports. Another edition, which will be designed for children, is being prepared.

All editions of Trivial Pursuit are played on the same board and make use of the same colored spaces in determining categories, but the categories that correspond to the colored spaces are different. A complete listing of the categories and colors follows:

Color	Genus	Baby Boomer
Brown	Art & Literature (AL)	Publishing (PUB)
Yellow	History (H)	Nightly News (NN)
Orange	Sports & Leisure (SL)	R.P.M. (RPM)
Blue	Geography (G)	Television (TV)
Green	Science & Nature (SN)	Lives & Times (LT)
Pink	Entertainment (E)	Stage & Screen (SS)

Color	Silver Screen	All-Star Sports
Brown	On Screen (ON)	Basketball (BKB)
Yellow	Off Screen (OFF)	Catch All (ALL)
Orange	Portrayals (POR)	Numbers (NBR)
Blue	Settings (SET)	Nicknames (NNM)
Green	Production (PRO)	Baseball (BBL)
Pink	Titles (TIT)	Football (FTB)

Questions and Answers Regarding the Game

The rules the manufacturer of Trivial Pursuit provides are quite brief and don't cover all game-playing situations. To assist you when you hit a trouble spot during gameplay, here are some of the most frequently asked questions players have regarding Trivial Pursuit.

Q. *How many people can play Trivial Pursuit?*

A. Although the makers of the game suggest that Trivial Pursuit is a game for two to twenty-four players, you can play solitaire—the rules are explained later in the book. You can also play the game with more than twenty-four players in tournaments. This tournament play is also discussed in the latter part of the book.

Q. *I know that the person who rolls the highest on the* *die goes first, but who goes second when starting the game?*

A. It's easiest to proceed counterclockwise, but if you want to have some tighter order, have the player who rolled second-highest go second, etc.

Q. *What's the best way to get a wedge out of a token when it's stuck?*

A. Try bouncing the wedge on a table. A few good bounces will get it out better than a knife would.

Q. *What if someone has won the game before other players have had a turn?*

A. The rules suggest that anyone who hasn't had a turn is entitled to a roll of the die. Here's a variation: Have the winning player become the gamemaster and read the questions for the rest of the game.

Q. *What's the easiest category in the Genus Edition?*

A. There is no single answer, although most people who aren't trivia buffs tend to find Entertainment somewhat easier and Geography somewhat more difficult than the other categories. Of course, if you tend to have knowledge in any specific category, you will find that category to be both your favorite one and the one that causes you the most stress. For more on ratings of categories, see Part Three of this book.

Q. *This doesn't relate to gameplay, but do you know why Trivial Pursuit is so expensive?*

A. Nope.

Q. *Who asks the questions?*

A. Obviously, anyone whose turn it is not. However, most players rotate this duty.

Q. *Isn't it better to have one player ask the questions?*

A. Absolutely not. Because of the strategies which can be employed by the reader, this gives one player an unfair advantage if he or she is good, or it gives the other players an unfair advantage if he or she is bad.

Q. *What kind of strategies?*

A. The kind of psychological terrorism reviewed later

in the text, in Part Four, "Psyching Out Your Opponent."

Q. *How frequently should the cards be rotated?*

A. Some players treat the questions like playing cards, passing the "deck" every turn. The problem with this is that each player then always gets questioned by the same other player, which can be an unfair advantage or disadvantage. It can also be time-consuming. Thus, it's common to find players turning over the reading chores every five rounds (that is, when each of the players has had five turns), giving everyone time to enjoy the lofty view from the catbird seat.

Q. *If someone doesn't want to compete but does want to take part, can that person be given the job of reading?*

A. Anyone can be reader, as long as no one carps when a novice happens to give someone an answer by singing a song title instead of reading it, by emphasizing a key word, and so forth. As you'll see later in the book, how you read the questions can be an important part of the game. On the other hand, since all players will benefit or be hurt by whatever qualities a single reader brings to the job, a nonplayer *can* be permitted to read the questions just for the sake of fellowship.

Q. *How exact do the answers have to be?*

A. This is one of the touchiest aspects of Trivial Pursuit. It's dismissed in the instructions as being governable by common sense, but one person's common sense is another's nitpicking. Some players demand that the complete answer be provided, and frequently the demand is justified. For example, if a question is about a Gershwin brother or one of the Redgrave sisters, the appropriate sibling should be identified. Also, if a question is about a specific historical event, say, the explosion of the *Hindenburg* or the *Thresher* tragedy, answering "a zeppelin" or "a submarine" is simply not sufficient.

Q. *What happens, though, if the reader okays an answer like "Gershwin," only to have one of the other* *players pipe up and demand, "Which Gershwin?"*

A. It's a fair request to make, and should not be looked upon as nitpicking. The person reading the question is not the final arbiter in these matters. At the same time, it should not be presumed that the person answering the question is trying to get away with something. For example, many proper nouns have become informalized in common usage. If someone identifies the former capital of Brazil as "Rio," chances are good that the player is not referring to Rio Cuarto or the Rio Grande, but to Rio de Janeiro.

Q. *Isn't there a point at which challenging an answer can be considered spoilsport tactics?*

A. It all depends on the way it's done. Let's face it: Some players can make a perfectly legal request with an *attitude* that makes you want to punch them. Which doesn't change the fact that they are within their rights asking for a more complete answer.

Q. *What's an example of being too nitpicky?*

A. If a player is asked to name the three astronauts killed in the Apollo 1 fire, an answer of Grissom, Chaffee, and White should be acceptable—even if the card says Gus Grissom, Roger Chaffee, and Edward White. The rule of thumb is this: *If the substance of an answer is clearly known, that is sufficient.*

Q. *What quantifies "substance"?*

A. In a nutshell (a walnut shell, for those who regard abbreviated references as shell games), substance is an answer which is spot-on, exactly what is requested, *or* is information from which the question can readily be guessed. In other words, the combination of Grissom, Chaffee, and White can only be the answer to the Apollo question, or one very much like it.

Q. *Forgive me, but that's still pretty vague.*

A. About the nutshell?

Q. *No, about the game.*

A. All right then, let's run through some instances which have arisen during gameplay. "Who resides at number 24 Sussex Drive in Ottawa?"

Q. *Pierre Trudeau?*

A. Common noun, please.

Q. *Uh . . . the President of Canada?*

A. Wrong. The Prime Minister of Canada.

Q. *Same thing!*

A. Not to the framers of the Canadian constitution.

Q. *But Trudeau does live there.*

A. Sorry. It didn't ask who lives there *now*.

Q. *Yes, but you said before that if someone knows the* substance *of an answer, like Grissom-White-Chaffee, that's good enough.*

A. In this case, "Trudeau" was just a small part of the answer, and "President" was dead wrong. That hardly qualifies as substance.

Q. *What you're saying, then, is that knowing something about an answer is not the same as knowing more or less what is required.*

A. Precisely. Here's another question to illustrate substance. "What was the headline of the New York *Times* on July 21, 1969?"

Q. *"Man Walks on Moon."*

A. Wrong. "Men Walk on Moon."

Q. *Same thing.*

A. Buzz Aldrin might not agree. Still, your answer is acceptable, since the essence of the question is *not* whether you memorized the front page of that particular newspaper, but whether you knew what had happened the day before.

Q. *What if an answer has some of the substance but is incomplete?*

A. You're out of luck. For instance, "What was dropped by *Bock's Car* in 1945?"

Q. *1945? It had to be an atom bomb.*

A. Where?

Q. *I don't know. But I know the* Enola Gay *bombed Hiroshima, so it must have been the second one dropped.*

A. That's still not enough. The answer is Nagasaki.

Q. *What happens when the card's answer is one of many?*

A. The reader is allowed to "appeal" to a higher reference authority. For example, "What's an opera's lead female singer called?"

Q. *A diva.*

A. The card says "prima donna," so you crack a dictionary just as you'd do in Scrabble™, Perquackey™, or any other fact-oriented game. And it tells us that a diva is a "prima donna," so your answer is correct.

Q. *Then the game answers aren't always the last word?*

A. Not by a long shot, which is elaborated upon in the section on incorrect answers in Part Three.

Q. *What happens if there's no dictionary handy?*

A. In that case, the player answering the question gets the benefit of the doubt and is offered another question.

Q. *And if that question is answered so easily that the other players cry "foul"—what then?*

A. Those are the breaks of the game. Besides, the chances are just as good that the player will get a real jawbreaker of a question; it all works out in the end.

Q. *What do you do if there are two correct answers, completely different, but it's clear to the reader which one is wanted?*

A. Assuming the reader is semi-intelligent, they should give the player another shot at the right answer. For example, "What did Dan Aykroyd and John Belushi do after leaving *Saturday Night Live*?"

Q. *They became movie actors.*

A. That's true. However, the answer the game wants is "They became the Blues Brothers." Now then, if the reader knew nothing about the comedians and told the answerer that he or she was wrong, the answerer would not be out of line to ask for another card. However, readers who are alert and moderately well read will do what's done on TV's *Family Feud* and say something like "Before that."

Q. *Couldn't other players complain that this is the equivalent of "leading the witness"?*

A. The only time they would be justified in feeling that way is if the reader said something overtly helpful like "No, but they acted in a movie about this." Otherwise, fair-minded players want to *test* their opponents, not cheat them with a question which happens to be vague. Here's another: "What play has been performed more than any other in British theater?"

Q. *Probably* Macbeth.

A. No, *The Mousetrap*. But the question didn't say *consecutive* run, so the player was understandably confused. If the reader didn't offer that clarification before announcing the answer, a new question is in order.

Q. *What happens if a reader accidentally prompts the player* beyond *the call of clarification?*

A. The other players will start shouting things like "*Shhhhh*" or "Why'd you say that, idiot?"

Q. *And what happens to the question?*

A. If the player still doesn't get the answer, the point is obviously moot. If the player does, the general practice is to ask a new question.

Q. *Even if the player knew the answer?*

A. No one, not even the player, will ever be entirely convinced of that. Remember, even a tiny or indirect nudge can jar an answer loose. To provide an extreme example, suppose the question is "What Greek letter describes the value 3.14?" And suppose, after posing the question, the reader innocently says, "Ohhh . . . so-and-so should have *no trouble* getting *that* one!" Now, assume so-and-so knows squat about math but happens to be a baker. Because of that clue, the player may put two and two—or in this case, 3.14 and 3.14—together and dredge "pi" from dim recollections of junior high math. Of course, if the player is a physicist, the other players may elect to be generous and let the question be played. But it's *their* choice, not that of the player.

Q. *Is a player also given a new question if he or she mishears what was asked?*

A. Only if a player honestly thought the question was something else entirely, such as "Who fell at Waterloo?" when it was really "Who fell at Watergate?" The answer should tip off the reader that something is amiss and the question should be reread.

Q. *What if the reader has already blurted out the answer?*

A. Then the player is entitled to try to show how the misheard question inspired the answer he or she gave. If the player can do so, a new question should be posed. This does *not*, however, apply to sloppy listening.

Q. *What's that?*

A. Answer this question: "Who slung a .44-40 hair-trigger-action rifle?"

Q. *The Rifleman, of course.*

A. No, Lucas McCain.

Q. *But he was the Rifleman!*

A. Perhaps, but that was the name of the *show*. The question specifically asked who, not in what show.

Q. *What about time limits? What's a fair amount of time for a player to answer a question?*

A. Thirty seconds. Indeed, one of the games mentioned later in this text, Trivia Adventure™, actually suggests that as a time limit for the game. Players shouldn't convolute the game by keeping a stopwatch at hand, but you can pretty well measure how much time has passed by the amount of fidgeting the other players are doing.

Q. *What if a player is asked to provide a different answer, as in a question such as the one about* The Mousetrap?

A. In that case, an additional fifteen seconds should be extended.

Q. *On another subject, are there any "illegal" rolls of the die?*

A. Yes. It's common practice in board games that a roll which goes partially or entirely off the board or leans even slightly against a token is discounted.

Q. *Some players like to play Trivial Pursuit in teams. What happens if teammates disagree on a correct answer?*

A. As in politics, the majority rules. If there's a split decision and no side will yield, the matter should *not* be settled through boring minutes of deliberation. After thirty seconds, the reader can order a roll of the die, with an even spin favoring one answer, odd the other.

Q. *Once in a while, players are asked questions they tackled in previous games. Are they obliged to tell the other players?*

A. If the player knew the answer in a previous game, he or she should be allowed to answer it again. If the player was *told* the answer, another question should be selected.

Q. *What if the player doesn't remember the answer?*

A. The player still gets another question. If he or she suddenly remember the answer, it will only be because it had been given once before. Trivial Pursuit is a test of awareness and deduction, not regurgitation.

Q. *What if you know a player is lying about having had a question?*

A. If players are willing to lie, they probably won't own up to having done so when confronted. Don't make a scene—just don't play with them again.

Q. *Speaking of making a scene, one of the biggest problems in Trivial Pursuit is deciding what constitutes a given answer. Are there any parameters?*

A. Not really, and it *is* a problem—since the reader by asking "Is that your answer?" can dramatically affect play. At the same time, there's the very real possibility that a player, while mulling over an answer, may mutter it openly, only to have an overzealous reader jump on it with a "Wrong!" That's unfair to the player, who may honestly not have been aware that he or she was thinking aloud. While most players treat an official "answer" as one which is stated affirmatively in a normal speaking voice, even when it's preceded by "I think it's..." or even an interrogative like "Is it...?" It's a good idea for the reader to say "Repeat, please," if there's any doubt.

Q. *What do you do if a reader gives the answer after having mistaken a player's out-loud thinking for a given answer?*

A. Again, the player answering the question gets the benefit of the doubt and a new question is read.

Q. *What if the player admits he or she wouldn't have gotten the answer?*

A. The player is still within his or her rights in requesting a new question. To repeat, in Trivial Pursuit an answer can come from the brain's left field at any time, even as another answer is being considered aloud.

Q. *Can a player change a given answer before the reader has had a chance to respond?*

A. No.

Q. *Even if the given answer was wrong and the player suddenly realized that?*

A. That's right. It's in the nature of the game for readers to reply quickly, with their expression and body language as well as with words. For a player to cry foul once the reader has reacted is both unreasonable and potentially incendiary. There's no reason a question shouldn't be thought through before replying.

Q. *What happens if you accidentally move another player's token or move the wrong number of spaces, taking a question before anyone catches the error?*

A. The question—and answer, if given—stand only if you end up on the same category once everything has been set aright. You shouldn't have had the question in the first place; so, right or wrong, it goes to the back of the pile.

Q. *Even if it hasn't been answered?*

A. Yes. Knowing what question to expect, other players will also know whether or not to avoid that category.

Q. *This isn't a point of order, but the rules say it's up to the players to decide whether to read a correct answer when a wrong one is given. What do you say?*

A. Read it. Though it's one fewer question those players can use in future games, it makes life less frustrating for inquisitive players. Besides, what would Trivial Pursuit be without the forlorn "Rats, I was *going* to say that," the self-reproachful "I should've *known* that," and the piteous "Damn. Never *heard* of the sucker."

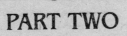

PART TWO

WINNING
BOARD STRATEGIES

There are two ways of approaching the Trivial Pursuit board: either keep general tactics in mind, or employ a wedge-by-wedge conquest strategy.

The advantage to the latter approach is that it's basically foolproof: If you use a patterned conquest strategy, you will know how to capture all the wedges with the least amount of idle roaming. Buffs of chess-type games will find these patterns particularly satisfying.

However, if you're one of those free spirits who prefers a less structured game of Trivial Pursuit, there are still fundamental board strategies you should acquaint yourself with. The dos and don'ts are as follows:

- *Do* opt for the move that will put you within one-throw striking distance of a headquarters containing one of the wedges you need. Do this even if the category isn't to your liking; you'll be amazed how much game time you waste pursuing favorable questions instead of ending your turn on a tough category.
- *Do*, for the most part, play the rim instead of the spokes: Those roll-again spaces are valuable. The exceptions are delineated below.
- *Don't* shun a headquarters with a tough category. You'll have to deal with it eventually, and it's better to do so while you're in the neighborhood. Remember, you can be four wedges behind another player and suddenly go on a roll.
- *Do* remember that closer to a headquarters is not

necessarily better. A throw of six is as likely to come up on the die as a throw of one.

- *Do* put as many roll-again spaces as possible between yourself and the headquarters, as long as you remain one throw away. It's better to be six spaces away with two of them roll-agains than four away with one roll-again.
- *Don't* go to a roll-again if it places you more than one throw away from a headquarters you need.
- *Don't* go to a wild-card hub just because you don't like a rim category. There are *five* category questions between the hub and any headquarters, as opposed to three category questions and two roll-agains on the rim.
- *Don't* strand yourself between remote headquarters in the latter stages of play: Select a target and hover as close as possible. "Deserts" of eleven spaces and upward between distant headquarters can be *very* unproductive.

While this overview will prove sufficient to get you through most of the choices which arise during gameplay, you would be wise to break out the board, six wedges, and a token, and walk through the tactics and situations described below. You needn't memorize these strategies, of course, but you *should* be able to recognize certain patterns when they occur. How you deal with them could mean the difference between moving surefootedly through the game or wandering aimlessly.

Opening Tactics

Whatever you roll on your opening move, the organization of the colors is such that you can land on a category of your choosing. Some players automatically move so that they are near the headquarters of their favorite category. Bad Idea.

It's best, on the opening roll, to go to the *category* you are best qualified to answer (the obvious exception being if you roll a six and can go right to the headquarters of your choosing). Answering this question leaves you within one toss of a headquarters.

Needless to say, wherever you are on *any* turn, if you can move to a roll-again space and stay within striking distance of a target, you should do so. Roll-again spaces serve two purposes:

1. They can move you into one-roll striking range of a headquarters without having to answer a question.
2. If you're already in range, they give you what amounts to two tries at getting onto the headquarters.

Your First Wedge

If you are positioned on the spoke and throw a number that gets you onto the rim but places you on neither the headquarters nor a roll-again space, one of three things will happen:

1. You will not spin high enough to leave the spoke. In that case, still try to move forward, since it will put you in reach of the roll-again spaces. If you go backward, you'll still be one roll from the headquarters, but with a lessened or nonexistent roll-again option. The only reason to go backward, especially as far back as the hub, is if the category behind is markedly better for you.

2. You can go back along the spoke, through the hub, to another spoke.
3. You can go to the rim.

In the last two cases, the rim move is, statistically speaking, your best bet. You leave yourself not only within striking distance of a headquarters wedge, but with one or two roll-again slots to fall back—or forward—on. The only reason *not* to go to the rim is, again, if you're much stronger with the spoke category. In that case, proceed through the hub and make, as your new objective, the headquarters that is now within one roll.

In terms of tactics, as long as the board is full of wedges, follow the roll-again segments wherever they carry you; regardless of where you are on the rim, you will always be within one-roll striking distance of a headquarters.

Your Second Wedge

After taking your first headquarters, you're at the equivalent of a fork in the road: You can remain on the rim or you can head for the hub.

At this stage of the game, the rim is still the best place to be. Rolling from the headquarters, a two or five will get you to a roll-again—odds of three to one. If you manage to buck those not overwhelming odds, you get a one-roll crack at a new wedge.

If you spin a one, three, four, or six, the odds shift for the better. When it's your turn to spin again, depending upon where you are, either four or five of the six numbers on the die will work in your favor:

1. If you're on a rim leg of a triad (the three identically colored spaces surrounding a headquarters), a one, four, or three puts you on a roll-again; a six gets you to a fresh headquarters.
2. If you're on the rim two segments from the triad of the conquered headquarters, a one, two, or five gets you to a roll-again; four puts you on a new headquarters.
3. Best of all, if you're on the rim three segments from the triad whose headquarters you have recently pillaged, a one, two, five, or six gets you a roll-again; a three puts you on another headquarters.

In the cases cited above, note that in each possible location, one of the roll-again spaces (the roll of three, five, and six, respectively) directs you *away* from the headquarters you have selected as your new destination. However, you are then five segments from another new headquarters—not to mention three and four spaces from roll-again spaces.

If you have elected to go onto the spokes this early, you achieve only one advantage, negligible at this time: access to the hub, and, hence, a throw of six from any of the remaining five headquarters. Before you move inside the wheel, consider that playing the rim, the odds are either four or five in six that you won't have to answer a question to get to the next wedge; playing the spokes, you will have to answer *at least* one question. Even if you roll a six, land on the hub, and get to choose your own category, you still risk missing it and surrendering your turn. Even if you answer the hub question, the odds are against spinning another six. That means you'll have to answer a second question before getting to roll for a new headquarters.

In short, stick to the rim. Even if the categories are

not to your liking, the odds of compensating for wrong guesses with roll-again spaces are in your favor.

Your Third Wedge

Once you have captured your second wedge, gameplay alters dramatically.

There are three patterns that can exist after a pair of headquarters has been taken:

1. A hemisphere pattern—four unconquered headquarters on one side of the board
2. An X arrangement—four unconquered headquarters at each base of the letter
3. A three-and-one setup—three unconquered headquarters neighboring each other, with another unconquered headquarters directly opposite

Let us look at these in turn.

HEMISPHERE PATTERN

If you have created a hemisphere pattern, that means you're already on the rim. Stay there and make for the next headquarters over, whether it's to the left or the right. Again, there are roll-again segments two and five moves in the direction you're headed; however, the roll-again spaces in the *other* direction lead you to a conquered headquarters.

While you're still on the headquarters you have just

earned a wedge from, this fact is irrelevant, since it takes a roll of two or five to reach *either* set of roll-again spaces. Getting one or the other number, you'll make for headquarters whose wedge you have not yet earned.

However, if you're already off the conquered headquarters, the roll-again situation becomes tricky.

Numerically speaking, all of the rolls mentioned above ("Your Second Wedge") still apply. However, not all of them will bring you closer to a wedge. To wit:

1. If you're on the triad leg in the direction you want to go, a toss of one or four gets you a roll-again—still within one-roll striking distance of a headquarters wedge you want.
2. If you're four spaces shy of your goal, a one (moving backward) or two accomplishes the same end.
3. If you're three spaces from your goal, the same figures, reversed, apply.

However, you can *also* reach roll-again spaces which take you *away* from the unconquered headquarters—toward one you have already conquered. Moving in that direction leaves you out of one-roll striking range of a headquarters you want. Odds-wise, the chance of jumping from one of these out-of-the-way places to a roll-again in the direction you originally wanted to go are one in six.

Even if you're hopelessly illiterate in a category, don't go camping on one of these remote roll-again spaces. Better to give the wrong answer and have to wait another turn to go for the headquarters—buffered by two nearby roll-again segments—then to be stranded in a wedgeless wasteland surrounded by questions and roll-agains, most of which lead you further from your destination.

X PATTERN

If you should find yourself in an X pattern, head for either of the two unconquered headquarters nearest the headquarters you just conquered. Both are seven segments away, and it doesn't matter which you select.

Reaching the nearest headquarters, you will play as if it and the other unconquered headquarters seven spaces away are the only ones in the game. The other hemisphere doesn't exist: Your game is twelve segments wide, defined by the roll-again space outside the triad of each occupied headquarters.

The one exception which follows *seems* to have some appeal under an unusual set of circumstances—but it's misleading and should be avoided.

Ideally, you'll remain in the six spaces or "arc" between the two headquarters. That will allow you to stay a one-roll strike away from either. However, by remaining in this region, you're depriving yourself access to two categories. Looking at the board, you'll notice that in any given arc there are only four of the six categories. The remaining two categories are the two headquarters. If you can't seem to get on the headquarters, and these categories happen to be particular strengths of yours, they can only be reached as follows:

1. Head for segment two of the spoke on the right; or travel four spaces beyond the occupied headquarters on the right.
2. Go to the bottom of the spoke on the left; or slide four spaces beyond the headquarters on that side.

If you decide to go for these spots, you're limiting your access to roll-again spaces, not to mention a one-roll strike against one of the unconquered headquarters. While you could conceivably get to the other unconquered headquarters on a single roll, the odds against that are six to one—not good.

Should you nonetheless want one of those two categories, at least be aware that you can't even *reach* a roll-again space from the second space on the left spoke; that from the right spoke the odds are one in six; and that the chances against you are six to two outside the arc on either side.

This matter of going outside the arc is particularly dangerous. If you have gone that far from your target headquarters, you may well decide to abandon that hemisphere altogether and move to the other side of the X. Unfortunately, if you don't hop from roll-again space to roll-again space—and even if you do hit one or two— you can well become mired in the nine-space desert between the two sides of the X, answering questions which, if you'd bothered to address them *within* the arc, would have left you in much better position to pounce on wedge-bearing headquarters.

In other words, it's better to tackle a tougher category and lose a turn than to chase after a safer subject and possibly squander many turns.

After you have captured one of the two wedges, you're seven spaces from the other one on that side of the X; that, abetted by two roll-again segments, leaves you in excellent field position.

THREE-AND-ONE PATTERN

If you find yourself faced with this beastly setup, go for the one headquarters that is by itself, treating the headquarters as though it were the only spot on the board you want to be on. Be patient: Use the roll-again spaces and, like Muhammad Ali in his prime, hover about your target stinging like a bee until it succumbs.

Whatever you do, though, stay off the spokes of the wheel. Heading toward the hub limits your ability to reach the roll-again spaces. For instance, you're on the rim, one space from the occupied headquarters. You toss a five. If you were to go up the spoke, to segment one, your next turn could reward you with a roll-again on a throw of six, or the headquarters with a spin of four. However, if you had moved through the headquarters along the wheel's rim, a throw of two or six on your next turn would get you a roll-again, and a four a stab at the wedge. Your chances of success are nearly 17 percent better on the rim. Then too, being on the spoke and landing on a category you hate if you proceed toward your original goal may compel you to turn in the other direction—which has the potential to be a colossal time-waster if all you roll is ones and twos.

Although there is no tactical advantage to cleaning up one hemisphere before migrating to the other, it will help you to keep your objectives clear. It's easier to work your strategies when the three remaining wedges are all in one place.

Your Fourth Wedge

With half the board cleared, you will have one of four patterns to face:

1. Y-shape—Your unconquered headquarters are in every-other-headquarters position.
2. y-shape—Two of your unconquered headquarters are next to each other.

3. Three abreast—You need to conquer three headquarters in a row.

Taking them in turn, the following strategies apply:

UPPERCASE Y-SHAPE

As the name implies, this pattern resembles an up-
percase Y, created by taking every other headquarters on
the board. There are thirteen rim spaces and eleven spoke
spaces between each wedge. In this situation, both the
rim and the spokes offer their own advantages. Because
you will begin your assault from a headquarters between
two wedges you need, stay on the rim. A throw of two
or five gets you a roll-again, and even a one, three, four,
or six gives you access to those roll-again segments.
There is only one exception: If you are on a conquered
headquarters and throw a six, you may go to the hub.
Do this only if the categories on the triad legs adjoining
either headquarters are likely to give you trouble. The
hub is an acceptable place from which to launch an attack:
A six will get you onto a headquarters, while any other
throw will at least give you your choice of three different
categories.

As in the three-and-one pattern described earlier, hover
around each wedge until it is taken.

LOWERCASE Y-SHAPE

This pattern resembles a lowercase y, the result of
having taken the wedges of the hemisphere pattern out
of order, or nipping off just one leg of the X layout.
Whichever development gave you your y, you will be

seven spaces from the bottommost wedge. There's no tactical advantage in going for this one first, although, again, it will tidy up your game to take it and then have only one-sixth of the board to deal with.

Treat it, again, as the only wedge on the board. Strategies for one-wedge play are explored in the section "Your Sixth Wedge."

THREE ABREAST

If you have been taking the wedges in domino fashion, one beside the other, you are seven spaces from one of the two outermost wedges of this formation. Play this, again, as though it were the one remaining wedge.

While it is true that by placing yourself on the arc between the central wedge and one of the outermost wedges you will increase your chances of landing on a headquarters, you want to avoid the wide-V formation described in "Your Fifth Wedge." More throws are wasted courting the two wedges in that pattern than in any other Trivial Pursuit setup.

Your Fifth Wedge

Your efforts in obtaining the fourth wedge will leave you facing one of three patterns:

1. The line—you need wedges opposite one another.
2. The narrow—You need wedges beside each other.
3. The wide—You need wedges on either side of a conquered headquarters.

As the adjectives attached to the V-patterns imply, the difference between them is in the width of the mouth. The wide V has two arcs, or thirteen spaces between headquarters, the narrow V has six. In the line setup—which you will face if you bungled your fourth wedge and conquered a Y-shape headquarters *other* than the foot—you must deal with headquarters directly opposite one another.

THE LINE PATTERN

Commencing your assault on the line, you will find yourself seven spaces from one headquarters and fourteen from the other along the rim; or twelve from either if you decide to travel the spoke to the hub and through it along another spoke.

Obviously, which path you take will depend upon your first spin. If you roll a two or five, you're going to stop on the roll-again spaces. That will leave you a roll of five or two from the closest headquarters.

If you throw a one or three, you will also proceed along the rim toward the wedge. These numbers will put you in the same categories whether you take the rim or spoke; better to have access to the roll-again spaces in the neighborhood of the headquarters (two roll-agains if you toss a one, three if the die comes up three).

A roll of four will give you a choice of two categories; take whichever you prefer.

Throwing a six is the only toss-up. If you go to the hub, you get a category of your choice, and you are within one-roll striking distance of either headquarters. However, there isn't a roll-again segment in sight. If you move along the rim, you can hit an occupied headquarters with a throw of one (there's also a roll-again one spin away, but you obviously wouldn't go there), or roll-again spaces with spins of four or three. The deciding factor is how you feel about the category on that headquarters triad. If you are reasonably comfortable with it, go there; the roll-again spaces are worth it. If you'd rather choose your category, go to the hub. There, at least, you'll have your choice of one of two categories on your next spin, since the layout of categories on each spoke is different.

THE NARROW-V PATTERN

This one's the best of all possible worlds.

If you're just coming off the foot of a Y-shape, head for the hub. There are voids thirteen and/or twenty spaces wide if you go along the rim; despite the presence of four and six roll-again spaces respectively, this journey can prove tedious and time-consuming. You'll find yourself backtracking just to hit some of the roll-again spaces and could conceivably end up stranded in a tough category far from your goal. Also, you'll be limited in the variety of categories from which you can choose. Conversely, once you hit the hub, you can select either spoke and its categories to reach one of the two remaining wedges; if you spin low, for example a two or three, you will also be able to backtrack: leave a spoke and go through the hub onto another spoke, still remaining in one-roll distance from an unconquered headquarters.

If you nab a wedge from either of these vantage points, great. If not, don't go *back* onto a spoke, but remain on the arc between the two headquarters. On the spoke, you'll be in one-roll range of only a single wedge.

Once you're in the arc, the perimeters of your hunting ground are the roll-again segments two spaces beyond the wedges. Again, if you don't accept these boundaries, you're courting disaster. For instance, if you were to roll a three while on one of these segments, your inclination might well be to move to the roll-again segments five spaces *away* from the wedges, hoping for a three or five on your next turn. *Don't!* The chances of success are two in six. On the other hand, going *toward* the central wedge, you are a throw of one or six from a headquarters, not to mention three and four spaces from a roll-again. Although you'll have to take a question, even if you get it wrong, your next turn gives you a four-in-six chance of hitting a roll-again space. Good odds.

THE WIDE-V PATTERN

This setup is marginally worse than the line.

With the line, there is no question but that you're going to travel along the spokes of the wheel. Here, your temptation may be to stay on the rim of the wheel with its prize of roll-agains; however, this has the potential of being a monumental time-waster.

The wide V is created by taking one of the top wedges from the Y-shape, or snatching the central wedge from three-abreast. Of the two, the three-abreast scenario is the most favorable. You're between the unconquered headquarters, and though you're not within one-roll striking distance, you have the option of taking one of two arcs which, except for the triad and roll-again segments, offer different arrangements of categories.

Needless to say, play one headquarters at a time. Don't abandon one for the other: You'll need a remarkable streak of luck to hit roll-again segments and make the trip in one turn. Play it as the only wedge on the board.

If you're out in left field because you've pillaged the wrong end of the Y-shape, you should move along the rim *unless* you roll a six. With a six, while most players still prefer the wheel's rim, it's not a runaway favorite. A six will put you on a triad along the rim, or else on the hub. Question-wise, the hub obviously has the edge. Then, too, whatever you roll on the next turn, you can choose from two categories, since the layouts, again, are different along either spoke. Even after that, you can go from one spoke, through the hub, to the other spoke if the category there is better for you. You'll still be within one-roll range of an occupied headquarters.

The disadvantage, obviously, is that you can't reach a single roll-again space from the hub. While a roll of six from the conquered headquarters will deposit you on the near leg of the triad surrounding your target headquarters, you may want to take your chances with the question and thereafter have access to three roll-again spaces; the alternative is the question-only spokes.

Your Sixth Wedge

Depending upon which pattern you had to deal with for your fifth wedge, your position relative to the last unconquered headquarters is as follows:

1. Narrow V—You are seven rim spaces or twelve spoke spaces away.
2. Wide V—You are fourteen rim spaces or twelve spoke spaces away.
3. Line—You are twenty-one rim spaces or twelve spoke spaces away.

In all but the line situation, if you spin a two or five, take the wheel's rim route. Those are roll-again spaces, and in the case of the narrow V you'll be in one-roll striking distance from the last wedge. If you toss a one, again the rim is recommended: either way puts you on a triad leg and, hence, the same question category. However, the rim thereafter gives you a two-in-six chance of a roll again. Throwing a three also puts you on the same category whether you go rim or spoke: Here, the rim is far superior, since you can reach one of three roll-again spaces on your next roll. Where you go with a four depends solely on the category you prefer. With a six, proceed to the next triad over if that's your favorite category; otherwise, move to the hub.

If you have just dealt with one end of the line layout, consider the rim *only* if you toss a five. That roll-again segment reduces your journey from twenty-one to sixteen spaces, four of those roll-agains. On the other hand, if you're comfortable with the category five spaces along the spoke, take that instead. You'll be seven segments from the occupied headquarters. There'll be no way of getting around answering a question. However, you'll be left within one-roll striking distance of the wedge. With a bit of bad luck, going the rim route could require as many as *eleven* turns to reach your destination! Following a roll of five, a worst possible scenario along the spokes is a more tolerable seven turns.

Regardless of the route you take, once you're on either of the arcs or the spoke bordering the final unconquered headquarters, there are clear tactics to follow. We've been alluding to the "last remaining wedge" situation throughout this chapter, and here's what it's all about.

The most important point to keep in mind is that you must avoid the tendency to practice what we often do in other board games—that is, the instinct to get as close as possible to the headquarters you need. "Striking distance" and "as close as possible" are not necessarily synonymous; indeed, they can be contradictory.

Let's say you find yourself on one of the rim segments of your target headquarters' triad. You throw a five on the die. Your inclination may be either to move onto the spoke or else to go through the headquarters so that you're four spaces distant on the other side. However, the wisest move is actually to go *away* from the headquarters. That would leave you a roll of six from the headquarters— but with two roll-again spaces between you and your objective. The odds of spinning a six, one, or four—the latter two being the roll-agains—are greater than those of spinning useful (i.e., non-question) numbers along the other two routes; that is, a two or four had you gone through the headquarters, or a four on the spoke.

The same philosophy holds true if you happen to be on the spoke segment of a triad whose wedge you must gather. If you roll a four and the subject of the category is not really an issue, *don't* back toward the hub; go onto the rim. That course will leave you with a roll-again space between you and the headquarters. If you don't spin the three you need to get in, you may be lucky enough to throw a one and get a second crack at the wedge.

A slightly different situation would be if you were four spaces from the elusive wedge and you happened to spin a three. You *could* move to the nearest segment of the headquarters triad, leaving yourself one move from the wedge; or you could retire to the headquarters behind you. If you're more confident of answering the headquarters question, go to it. Although you will be out of one-roll range of your objective, there are two roll-again spaces: The odds in favor of spinning a two and earning another throw—with three (roll-again) or five (wedge) useful thereafter—are better than those of tossing a one and sliding right into the headquarters.

In short, push from your mind the reflexive one-segment-away-is-better-than-six-away perception of the board. As long as you stay within *one-roll* striking distance of your goal, only the strength of the category and the roll-again segments determine the best course of action.

Winning

The object of Trivial Pursuit is to get to the hub (or center) in order to pit yourself against the game-winning question. You are free to head for the hub after you have collected wedges of each color. But what happens if you get there, elated and raring to go, and you botch the job by getting the answer wrong? You must leave the hub, of course, and return to it for a second go. Stay on the spokes, always moving to a strong category.

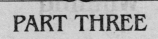

PART THREE

WINNING
CARD STRATEGIES

What is at once wonderful and frustrating about Trivial Pursuit is that all the board strategy in the world isn't going to help if you can't answer the questions. Trivial Pursuit is truly a game for statisticians as well as tacticians.

Few among us are going to shine in every category, or in every subcategory within a category. You may select the Genus Edition's Entertainment category because you're confident of your knowledge about movies; but, alas, you're almost as likely to draw a question about opera, the Beatles, or TV Westerns. Going with a seemingly safe category *isn't* always the best strategy in Trivial Pursuit. For example, suppose you're a whiz at basketball trivia, but know nothing about any other sport. In the Genus Edition, there are only twenty-three basketball questions in the set of 1,000: The rest of the Sports & Leisure category has to do with everything from wine to the roller derby.

As we saw in Part Two on board strategies, any roll of the die will usually give you the choice of landing on one of two different categories. It will help you to make a better decision where to go if you're more alert to the kinds of questions you'll be facing. The following overview will allow you to do that, at a glance, for each of the twenty-four categories in the various card sets of Trivial Pursuit.

Players will find the breakdowns useful in another way. It's been the author's experience—when trying to persuade the timorous to play Trivial Pursuit—that being able to *show* leery friends subcategories in which they may be proficient is more persuasive than whining, hectoring, or calling them party poopers. That, along with a comforting lie like "You'll be surprised how much you *do* know," should do the trick.

How to Determine Your Strongest Category

For all its impression of abundance, Trivial Pursuit favors the decade of the 1960s to the extent that questions that arise from that decade are twice as abundant as those from any other era. Between them, the 1960s and 1970s monopolize more questions than all other historical periods combined. Though older players may feel discriminated against, the game-buying market is dominated by adults in their twenties and thirties. Thus, one must forgive the creators' marketing orientation.

On the other hand, the prejudices *within* those eras are something else altogether. Here, as both a consumer's guide and strategy overview, is an analysis of what you can expect and should beware of, edition by edition, category by category. A one-to-four-star rating is used to indicate how diverse and difficult the categories are. A single star for difficulty indicates that the category is extremely easy. Four stars for diversity indicates that the category is extremely diverse in the kinds of questions asked.

GENUS EDITION

All in all, Genus is the most party-oriented of the Trivial Pursuit editions. Questions are equally distributed between the knowable, the clued, and the picayune, with categories that cater more even-handedly than any other to players of all age groups and interests.

Sports & Leisure (SL)

Considering their relative popularity, the scarcity of football questions—when contrasted with the number about baseball—is the most curious bias of Trivial Pursuit.

This imbalance aside, SL is one of the most variegated Trivial Pursuit categories. There are 142 distinct *subcategories*; though the category is dominated by the enduring spectator sports baseball, football, basketball, and hockey, as well as such popular pastimes as jogging, golf, and tennis, "miscellaneous" pursuits are the largest single subcategory, with 24.6 percent of all the questions. These miscellaneous questions include stumpers on Chinese checkers, knitting, mumbletypeg, horseshoes, skateboarding, rodeo, amusement parks, hunting, shuffleboard, the soapbox derby, weightlifting, fishing, scuba diving, coin and stamp collecting, perfumes, roller-skating, lotteries, curling, earthball, etc.

You're going to get a lot of these miscellaneous questions wrong, though when you hear the answers most will be familiar; withal, SL is one of the game's most eclectic and entertaining categories.

Diversity: ★★★
Difficulty: ★★★

Topic	Percentage of Questions
Baseball	11.2
Cards	5.5
Horse Racing	5.4
Liquor	5.1
Golf	4.9
Pro Football	4.8
Boxing	4.6
Olympics	
General	3.9
Specific Events	3.4
Tennis	3.6
Gambling	3.3
Basketball	2.3
College Football	2.3
Car Races	2.3
Boating	2.3
Food	1.9
Scrabble	1.7
Monopoly	1.6
Hockey	1.5
Chess	1.4
Billiards	1.1
Soccer	1.0

Geography (G)

Even if a player happens to know answers to questions about states which don't border their own—most of us don't—Trivial Pursuit digs deep into the geographical treasure chest to humble us all. It isn't enough to ask which states adjoin California or New York; the authors pose questions about the Scripps Institution of Oceanography, West Quoddy Head in Maine, and the city which has the most chapels per capita.

Doubly unfortunate is that this category doesn't even devote the majority of its questions to the United States, which is at least vaguely familiar to most of us. Your chances of going abroad with an even less pleasant question are a hefty 60 percent. Yet, most unfortunate is that even if you *are* familiar with world geography, including out-of-the-way places like the South Pole (two questions) and the Canary Islands (just one), that's hardly a guarantee of success. You may well know whether Marseille, France, is on the Atlantic or Mediterranean, or if Alaska and Hawaii are in the same or different time zones. But have you a foggy notion where Kruger National Park is located, or what landmark possesses 1,792 steps?

By consensus, Geography is the most difficult of all the Genus Edition categories. Moreover, it's lenient with no one; young and old are crushed with equal impunity.

Diversity: ★★★
Difficulty: ★★★★

Place	*Percentage of Questions*
United States	32.1
Europe	30.1
South America	5.0
Middle East	4.5
Africa	3.7
Bodies of Water	3.1
Russia	2.9
India	2.2
Far East	2.0
Canada	1.9
Australia	1.9
Scandinavia	1.7

Art & Literature (AL)

More than any other Genus category, Art & Literature and Entertainment are overstocked with their authors' pet subjects. Everywhere you turn there's a question about James Bond, *Playboy* magazine, Sherlock Holmes, or Superman. *Playboy* actually edges out *Time* magazine for having the most questions of any magazine or newspaper, while *Penthouse* takes third place. As far as AL is concerned, *Newsweek*, *Sports Illustrated*, *Psychology Today*, and *Grit* don't exist. Yet, culture lovers have an even greater shock in store: In the area of contemporary literature, books by John Updike, Truman Capote, Norman Mailer, John Hersey, James Michener, and a dozen other real writers combined don't come close to Erich Segal's *Love Story* and Peter Benchley's *Jaws*, which, between them, share over 10 percent of the questions.

Diversity: ★
Difficulty: ★★

Topic	Percentage of Questions
Literature	
Contemporary	12.1
1900–1950	11.4
19th-century	9.1
pre-19th-century	1.3
Biographies	5.6
Authors	5.6
Periodicals	5.2
Nonfiction	4.6
Artists	4.2
Comic Strips	4.1

Topic	Percentage of Questions
Myths and Folklore	3.3
Bible	3.2
Foreign Words	3.1
Plays	3.1
Nursery Rhymes	2.5
Punctuation and Language	2.5
Shakespeare	2.0
Poetry	1.9
Comic Books	1.8
Fairy Tales	1.7
James Bond	1.4
Sherlock Holmes	1.4
Gone with the Wind (novel)	1.3
Alice in Wonderland	1.1
Peanuts	1.1
Playboy	1.1
Literary quotes	1.0

Entertainment (E)

As mentioned earlier, the authors of Trivial Pursuit go again and again to a few pet subjects, specifically *Gone with the Wind, Jaws, The Poseidon Adventure, The Russians Are Coming, The Russians are Coming!,* and *The Godfather.*

However, many players mistakenly assume that this category is devoted primarily to movies. While there *are* a lot of movie questions—474, to be exact—there are 526 *non*-movie queries. Chances are a little better than even that you *won't* be asked about the silver screen. And even if you are, the subcategories are neatly scattered across the tinsel rainbow. Still, fans of ballet and opera must content themselves with a paltry seven questions, country-music buffs with six. The remaining one-of-a-kind queries—bulking out to a total of 2.8 percent of the questions—cover everything from the Muppets to the identity of the Ivory Soap baby.

Diversity: ★★
Difficulty: ★★

Topic	Percentage of Questions
Movies	
Actors and Roles	15.4
'60s	6.4
Stars' Private Lives	5.9
Oscars	5.1
'70s	3.1
'50s	2.1
Music	2.0
Miscellaneous	1.9
Quotes	1.7
'40s	1.3
'30s	1.2
1900–1920	0.8
'80s	0.5
TV shows	
'50s	6.3
'60s	3.7
Westerns	3.0
Miscellaneous	1.8
'70s	1.7
Game Shows	1.4
Mary Tyler Moore Show	1.0
Star Trek	0.8
Stars' Private Lives	0.6
Tonight Show	0.6
News	0.6
Quotes	0.5
'80s	0.2

Topic	Percentage of Questions
Music	
'60s	4.5
1900–1949	4.2
'50s	2.8
'70s	2.1
Beatles	1.8
Pre-20th-century	0.4
Comedians and Entertainers	3.0
Theater	2.6
Cartoons	2.5
Radio	1.2

Science & Nature (SN)

Few subjects intimidate more people than science. And while SN might not be quite as pleasant as a day at the beach, it's far more merciful than you would expect. Physics and chemistry have been held to a minimum; conversely, a great deal is seen of the human body, and disease runs rampant.

Surprisingly, computers are the subject of a measly four questions, while the dinosaurs are virtually extinct with but a single question in 1,000. Museums, organizations, photography, and broadcasting also make weak showings with five questions or less.

Purists have every right to quarrel with the inclusion of astrology, superstition (five questions), and monsters (three) in Science & Nature. However, by stretching the parameters of SN, the authors of Trivial Pursuit have likewise expanded its appeal and accessibility. Indeed, if you're a housewife or househusband playing Trivial Pursuit against an Einstein, you actually have an advantage: Questions about weights, measures, and kitchen utensils far outnumber queries about the logarithms of light.

In short, don't be afraid of this category. It's kinder than you think.

Diversity: ★★★★
Difficulty: ★★★

Topic	Percentage of Questions
Disease/Medicine	7.5
Mammals	7.1
Distance/Measures	7.0
Human Body	6.5
Food and Drink	6.4
Terminology	5.8
Stars/Planets	5.1
Scientists	3.8
Space Travel	3.6
Inventions	3.1
Birds	3.0
Math and Numbers	2.8
Abbreviations and Symbols	2.8
Metals/Minerals	2.3
Insects	2.3
Astrology	2.1
Geology	2.1
Weather	2.0
Cats and Dogs	1.8
The Calendar	1.8
Chemistry	1.7
Flora	1.6
Physics	1.6
Miscellaneous Animals	1.5
Fish	1.1
Quotes	1.0
Books	1.0

History (H)

History is more or less a mini Genus Edition by itself. There are questions on entertainment: Straining the definition of history to its maximum, Trival Pursuit asks about Dinah Shore, Paul McCartney, Judy Garland, Joan Crawford, Carol Burnett, Elvis, Ringo Starr, Bing Crosby, Elizabeth Taylor, and Humphrey Bogart—twice each!— and Marilyn Monroe four times. Also highly visible are science (in the form of historical inventions, weaponry, aircraft, ships, etc.), geography (battle sites, location of nations, and so on), and literature (the Bible, books written by politicians, and the like). Only sports have been given short shrift, with a few scattered queries about games enjoyed by certain world leaders.

If there are any surprises, they lie in what the category does *not* contain. Except in connection to the Second World War, there is nothing about Japan, while fewer than three or four questions each are posed about China, Italy, Africa, and, most surprisingly, Eastern Europe. Occidentalists should find this all very heartening.

Regarding World War II, the preponderance of questions is to be expected. Not only does that war offer a rich mine of trivia, but the Second World War had an ethical imperative that makes it less downbeat than most other conflicts. Though Vietnam has a comparatively high profile in the Baby Boomer Edition, the questions in Trivial Pursuit were not designed to promote gloom and sorrow, but what our ally Mr. Shakespeare lovingly called "trifles light as air."

Diversity: ★★★
Difficulty: ★★

Topic	*Percentage of Questions*
U.S. Presidents	12.3
United Kingdom	7.7
Quotes	6.4
United States	5.7
World War II	5.3
JFK	4.7
Crime (excluding assassination)	4.6
Explorers	3.8
Germany	2.7
Abbreviations and Nicknames	2.5
France	2.2
Russia	2.1
Middle East	2.1
Organizations	1.8
World War I	1.8
U.S. Military (noncombat)	1.6
History B.C.	1.6
Finance	1.6
Disasters	1.5
U.S. (1960–present)	1.3
South America	1.2
State and Local	1.1
Europe	1.0
India	1.0
U.S. (1900–1960)	1.0
Law and Lawyers	1.0
Watergate	1.0
Black History	1.0
United Nations	1.0

BABY BOOMER

Contrasted with the Genus Edition, Baby Boomer strives to be a cornucopia of post–World War II trivia.

This is both good and bad. It's good because the battle-ground is clearly defined; it's bad because in half the categories—those dealing with the arts—the authors don't even try to contain their enthusiasm for personal favorites.

Television (TV)

Considering that virtually all of TV history exists within the baby boomer years, the emphasis on select shows is curious. Fifteen TV programs account for 19.6 percent of the questions—a large slab indeed. Add Ed Sullivan, Phil Silvers, and the *Tonight* show (which accounts for the bulk of the talk-show questions) and the proportion rises to more than 25 percent! Lost in the shuffle are many of the top-ten-rated shows of the past thirty-odd years, among them *Three's Company*, *Little House on the Prairie*, *Eight Is Enough*, *Sanford and Son*, *Adam 12*, *Sonny and Cher*, *Family Affair*, *Wild, Wild West*, Milton Berle, Arthur Godfrey, and countless others. Less than 0.2 percent of the questions deal with TV in the '80s—another inexplicable oversight.

TV buffs take note: this category is fun but terribly lopsided.

Diversity: ★★
Difficulty: ★★★

Topic	Percentage of Questions
'60s sitcoms	10.1
Game Shows	7.6
Variety	6.7
Westerns	6.4
'60s Drama	6.3
'50s Drama	5.9
News	4.3
'70s Drama	4.2
'70s Sitcoms	3.7
Children's Shows	3.2
Cartoons	3.0
'50s Sitcoms	3.0
Disney	2.9
Talk Shows	2.6
Ed Sullivan	2.6
Soap Operas	2.2
M*A*S*H	2.0
Mary Tyler Moore Show	1.8
Star Trek	1.3
Saturday Night Live	1.3
Phil Silvers' Shows	1.3
Honeymooners	1.3
Dick Van Dyke Show	1.3
Beverly Hillbillies	1.3
The Fugitive	1.2
Laugh-in	1.1
All in the Family	1.1
Man from U.N.C.L.E.	1.0
Leave It to Beaver	1.0
The Networks	0.9
Barney Miller	0.9
Superman	0.9
Batman	0.9
PBS	0.3

Topic	Percentage of Questions
Miniseries	0.3
Religious	0.2

Records (RPM)

Though more balanced than TV, RPM has its oversights too, among them the neglect of Neil Diamond, Bette Midler, Sonny and Cher, and others; while Roy Orbison is important, the average player will not feel that this country singer deserves twice as many questions as Barbra Streisand. Punk and jazz are also slighted, whereas Crosby, Stills, Nash and Young, Elton John, and the Beach Boys get more than their fair share.

There are some interesting questions about foreign musicians, folksingers, rock quotes, and Motown (which makes up nearly 70 percent of the black music questions). In summary, this is a category for fans of '60s rock.

Diversity: ★★★
Difficulty: ★★★

Topic	Percentage of Questions
'60s Groups	16.1
Beatles	12.7
'50s Groups	7.5
'50s Singers (singles)	6.1
'70s Singers (singles)	5.8
'60s Singers (singles)	5.5
'70s Groups	5.2
Black Music (post-'50s)	4.9
Folk	3.1
Rolling Stones	2.6
TV Music	2.6
Country	2.1

Topics	Percentage of Questions
Bob Dylan	1.9
Simon and Garfunkel	1.9
Beach Boys	1.5
Crosby, Stills, Nash	1.4
Composers (contemporary)	1.3
Elvis	1.3
American Pie	1.2
'50s Crooners	1.1
'80s Singers (singles)	1.1
Elton John	1.0
'60s Crooners	0.9
'40s Crooners	0.8
Instrumentals	0.6
Children's Songs	0.5
Gospel	0.3
Punk	0.3
Reggae	0.2
Jazz	0.1

Publishing (PUB)

As in Art & Literature, the stress on certain characters and works can be frustrating. Superman, James Bond, Batman, Archie, *Playboy*, and Wonder Woman appear often, while there is very little on romance, dictionaries, travel guides, plays, and foreign books. The dearth of questions about finance books, management treatises, cat books, and exercise regimens is especially puzzling given their long domination of the best-seller charts.

For the most part, while it lacks depth in the areas of literary and nonfiction questions, PUB is sufficiently pop-culture-oriented to please most players.

Diversity: ★★
Difficulty: ★★★

Topic	Percentage of Questions
Novels	
1961–present	13.3
1940–1960	5.1
1900–1939	0.8
Pre-20th-century	1.0
Magazines and Newspapers	14.7
Comic strips	11.4
Autobiographies	5.0
Nonfiction and History	4.3
Philosophy	3.3
Comic Books	3.3
Superman Comics	2.8
Biographies	2.8
J.R.R. Tolkien	2.3
James Bond	2.1
How-to	1.9
Children's Novels	1.8
Batman Comics	1.5
Wonder Woman Comics	1.5
Sex Books	1.3
Poetry	1.3
Archie Comics	1.2
Authors' Lives	1.0
Catalogs	1.0
Cookbooks	0.8

Stage & Screen (SS)

This category is far and away more evenly distributed throughout its subcategories than TV, RPM, and PUB. A wide variety of movie genres is covered, the stage is not slighted—nor is Broadway overemphasized—and even documentaries, nightclubs, and X-rated films get their day in the sun.

While foreign films don't get as much attention here as they do in the marketplace, this is a minor quibble.

Diversity: ★★★
Difficulty: ★★

Topic	Percentage of Questions
Movies	
'30s	0.5
'40s	0.5
'50s	4.0
'60s	10.5
'70s	12.0
'80s	1.0
Theater and Broadway	18.0
Rock and Roll	
Film	2.6
Concerts	9.6
Comedians	10.4
Science Fiction Films	10.0
Disney	2.3
Oscars	2.0
Horror Films	1.7
Animated Cartoons	1.6
Movie Documentaries	1.4
Clubs and Concert Halls	1.4
James Bond	1.0
X-rated Movies	1.0
Country Music	0.7
Foreign Films	0.5

Nightly News (NN)

There are over fifty subcategories with two or more questions, and while significant topics such as the women's movement, ecology, and the Soviet Union are slighted, the questions are for the most part evenly distributed among the rest of the subcategories.

Moreover, most of the questions are based on well-known news stories. The biggest problems in NN seem to occur with the space-program questions, which ask players to identify various missions by the names of the vessels. In general, however, anyone even passingly acquainted with current events will have a good chance of scoring here, and should go to this category whenever possible—if not for a challenge, then for a respite.

Diversity: ★★★★
Difficulty: ★★

Topic	Percentage of Questions
U.S. Presidents	18.4
Outer Space	7.7
Crime	6.9
JFK	6.7
Watergate	5.3
Vietnam	4.8
Black History	4.2
Disasters	2.9
Middle East	2.6
Congress, Governors, and Mayors	2.4
U.K.	2.4
Military (noncombat)	2.4
Counterculture	2.1
Religion	2.1
Eastern Europe	1.8
Charles Manson	1.8
RFK	1.6
Korean War	1.6
Prizes	1.3
Ted Kennedy	1.3

Topic	Percentage of Questions
Medicine and Diseases	1.3
Africa	1.3
Women's Movement	1.0
Central and South America	1.0
Russia	1.0

Lives & Times (LT)

Here's a switch: Hugh Hefner is snubbed, the astronauts make only a token appearance, and everyone *else* finally gets a turn in the spotlight—including Charles and Di, fast-food magnates, clothes designers, toymakers, prominent figures in industry, and so on. In short, people that every Trivial Pursuit player should know are asked about in this category.

Because of its familiarity, LT is a relatively easy category; its fun quotient is low (hence the low difficulty rating) but, strategically, it's one notch above a roll-again space.

Diversity: ★★★★
Difficulty: ★

Topic	Percentage of Questions
Rock and Roll	11.3
Presidents	9.5
Advertising	8.7
Food	7.3
Kennedys	4.0
TV	3.6
TV stars	3.4
Governors/Mayors	3.3
Counterculture	3.2
Non-rock Music	3.1

Topics	Percentage of Questions
Business and Industry	3.0
Beatles	2.9
Drugs	2.6
Medicine	2.6
Watergate	2.6
Women's Movement	2.3
Language	2.2
Sports	2.1
Space	2.1
Crime	1.9
Fashion	1.6
Black History	1.4
Cold War	1.3
Toys and Games	1.3
Magazines	1.0
Charles and Diana	0.9

ALL-STAR SPORTS

This edition of Trivial Pursuit is just what the sports buff ordered. What's more, if nonfans can gravitate toward NNM, ALL, and NBRS, they stand a chance of making an honorable showing.

Nicknames (NNM)

Like Sports & Leisure in the Genus Edition, this category manages a grand slam, touching many, many bases. While certain sports dominate (baseball, football, hockey, basketball, and boxing account for over half the questions), and a few sports are unfairly relegated to the bench (soccer and tennis score surprisingly low), 29.6 percent of the questions (nearly one-third) favor neither the sports buff nor the novice by dipping into darts, wrestling, cards, and other nonjock categories.

Even the questions about baseball, football, and basketball are relatively temperate, the difficult ones being reserved for their own subcategories.

Diversity: ★★★★
Difficulty: ★★

Topic	Percentage of Questions
Basketball	20.3
Baseball	11.1
Football	10.7
Boxing	7.5
College Football	6.9
College Basketball	3.6
Golf	3.0
Soccer	
U.S.	2.3
Europe	0.5
Cars/Motorcycles	2.2
Olympics	1.2
Bowling	1.1

Catch All (ALL)

Since there isn't a separate category for hockey, it's no surprise to find the category ALL pucked-up. More than one fifth of the questions are about this sport; if you know absolutely nothing about hockey, you might want to avoid this category.

However, like NNM, once you get past the biggies—in this case, hockey, boxing, tennis, and horse racing, accounting for 48 percent of the questions—the remaining subcategories are nicely dispersed among such attractions as chess, swimming, lacrosse, karate, cricket, and the like.

Diversity: ★★★★
Difficulty: ★★

Topic	Percentage of Questions
Hockey	21.8
Boxing	10.2
Olympics	
Summer	6.9
Winter	3.3
General	2.6
Tennis	8.9
Horseracing	7.1
Golf	7.0
Basketball	5.3
Cars/Motorcycles	5.1
Bowling	1.8
Football	1.1
Billiards	1.0

Numbers (NBR)

Of the three miscellaneous categories, Numbers most favors the pop-sports expert: The big four subcategories once again rule the roost, this time by a commanding 66.6 percent. However, most gamers will be equally challenged by the other 34.4 percent of the questions, which are scattered through ten major (1 percent and over) and over thirty minor categories, which include rodeo, wrist-wrestling, Ping-Pong, and even Trivial Pursuit.

Diversity: ★★
Difficulty: ★★★

Topic	Percentage of Questions
Baseball	22.8
Basketball	17.6
Football	16.2
Hockey	10.0
Olympics	
Summer	3.1
Winter	1.1
General	0.9
College Basketball	4.0
College Football	3.8
Golf	3.4
Boxing	1.8
Cars/Motorcycles	1.7
Bowling	1.3
Horse Racing	1.2
Stadiums	1.0
Soccer	0.9

Basketball (BKB)

Unless you're a devotee of basketball, closely following at least one team (hence, by association, most others), skip BKB. In fact, this is perhaps the most difficult category, since basketball gets far less mainstream news coverage than baseball and football. The novice may pick up some ambient information about the latter two; not so basketball.

Compounding the problem is the fact that the even less visible college games make up nearly one quarter of the questions. There are no free throws here.

For the buff:

Diversity: ★★★
Difficulty: ★★★

For the novice:

Diversity: ★
Difficulty: ★★★★

Topic	Percentage of Questions
College	24.2
Legendary Careers (non-centers)	13.4
History	
Pre-1960	3.3
Post-1960	6.3
Coaches	8.8
Centers	8.7
Pro Records	6.1
Playoffs	5.1
Owners/Commissioners	4.0
Media	1.9
Women	1.9
Statistics and Rules	1.8
Draft	1.4
Symbols and Insignia	1.1
Olympics	1.0
Referees	1.0
All-Star Games	1.0

Football (FTB)

Contrasted with BKB, FTB will give nonaddicts a chance to succeed. Not *much* of a chance, mind you—but you may be able to pull out a few questions about the Superbowl, stadiums, and well-known players/coaches like Joe Namath, Jim Brown, and Vince Lombardi.

For the buff:

Diversity: ★★★★
Difficulty: ★★

For the novice:

Diversity: ★★
Difficulty: ★★★

Topic	Percentage of Questions
College Football	19.7
Quarterbacks	10.3
Coaches	9.4
History	
Pre-1960	5.9
Post-1960	1.0
Superbowl	6.7
Records	4.6
Stadium	4.4
Playoffs	3.8
Runners	3.4
Statistics and Rules	3.1
Hall of Fame	2.4
Canadian Football	2.2
Commissioners/Owners	2.2
Symbols and Insignia	2.1
Kickers	1.6
Media	1.0

Baseball (BBL)

Of the one-sport categories, BBL is the one most likely to disappoint the fans and please the newcomers. You're not asked to rattle off individual players' statistics; the questions focus more on broad and widely covered career achievements of well-known players such as Babe Ruth, Mickey Mantle, Roger Maris, Reggie Jackson, and so on.

Diehard fans will also be disappointed, because, with

all the grand old names of the game—Lou Gehrig, Stan Musial, Gil Hodges, Whitey Ford, Jackie Robinson—less than 10 percent of the BBL questions bother with the careers and games from the pre-'60s era.

For the buff:

Diversity: ★★
Difficulty: ★

For the novice:

Diversity: ★★★
Difficulty: ★★★

Topic	*Percentage of Questions*
Pitchers	15.2
Players' Careers	11.1
World Series	9.8
Managers	8.6
Players' Lives	6.4
Media	5.7
History	
Pre-1960	4.2
Post-1960	0.6
Records	4.5
Stadiums	4.0
Symbols and Insignia	3.0
Awards	2.6
Statistics and Rules	2.3
Babe Ruth	2.1
Owners	1.9
All-Star Teams	1.8
Spring Training	1.2
Umpires	1.0

SILVER SCREEN

This specialty edition will not be as satisfying to the moviegoer as All-Star Sports is to the athletic booster.

More than in any other edition, the decade of the 1960s runs away with the bulk of the questions. Not only does this decade top five of the six categories, but 1960s questions scattered throughout the other subcategories give the decade's films and stars one-quarter or more of every category. The decade of the 1970s is the clear runner-up, both subcategories dominated by the same films noted in the Genus Edition's Entertainment category.

Having said this, most of the questions deal with movies that the real film buff will have seen: *The Wizard of Ox*, *Casablanca*, *2001: A Space Odyssey*, *Cool Hand Luke*, the Crosby-Hope "Road" pictures, and other popular films each get a few turns at bat. Oddball entries about *The Amazing Colossal Man* and actors like Rip Torn and Dale Evans may throw even the heartiest fans, but not often enough to dampen their enthusiasm and pride.

Though teens and baby boomers will have an advantage because of the many 1960s films, a good time will be had by all. And nonbuffs will be able to answer a much higher percentage of questions than in All-Star Sports, since movies and their stars make headlines more often than sports and athletes.

Settings (SET)

This category deals with where and when movies take place. Players who *haven't* seen a lot of motion pictures will have a 10 percent chance of scoring well. For example, you wouldn't necessarily have to have seen *Judgment at Nuremberg* to know when the war trials took place, or *Robinson Crusoe on Mars* to take an educated guess that Death Valley provided the backdrops for the Martian surface.

For the buff:

Diversity: ★★★
Difficulty: ★★★

For the novice:

Diversity: ★★
Difficulty: ★★★★

Topic	Percentage of Questions
'60s Movies	21.7
'70s Movies	16.0
'50s Movies	13.6
'30s Movies	7.2
'40s Movies	6.1
Crime and Mystery	5.1
Musicals	4.9
War Films	4.7
Nonsilent Comedy	4.3
Horror Films	3.6
Westerns	3.4
Science Fiction	3.1
Foreign Films	1.8
Animated Cartoons	1.0
'20s Movies	0.4
'80s Movies	0.3

Titles (TIT)

As you'll notice, the subcategories in TIT are virtually identical to those found in SET. The one difference: This category is a piece of cake for the nondevotee. Given a line of dialogue which includes "Shangri-La," most people recognize it as belonging to *Lost Horizon*; "Want me to do your hair?" can only be from *Shampoo*. Even the less obvious questions aren't terribly challenging, such as "What 1974 disaster film shook up Charlton Heston?"

Buffs will walk through most of the questions, providing them, once again, with the equivalent of a roll-again space.

For the buff:

Diversity: ★
Difficulty: ★

For the novice:

Diversity: ★★★
Difficulty: ★★

Topics	*Percentage of Questions*
'60s Movies	21.2
'70s Movies	15.6
'40s Movies	11.4
'50s Movies	9.8
Nonsilent Comedy	6.9
Science Fiction	5.1
Musicals	4.9
Crime and Mystery	4.6
Westerns	3.9
War Films	3.3
'30s Movies	2.4
'80s Movies	2.4
Foreign Films	1.6
Horror Films	1.4
James Bond	1.3
Mysteries	1.2
'20s Movies	1.1

Topics	Percentage of Questions
Animated Cartoons	1.1

Off Screen (OFF)

If there's a Silver Screen category that is the equivalent of neutral ground, OFF is it. As the unusual structure of the chart below indicates, having seen a lot of movies and knowing their plots, dialogue, and characters won't help as much as having read *People* magazine each week.

Because of its ample reservoir of subcategories—literally hundreds, many with only one or two questions each—this is at once the most eclectic and the most entertaining Silver Screen category.

Diversity: ★★★★
Difficulty: ★★★

Topic	Percentage of Questions
Eras:	
'50s	6.6
'40s	6.4
'70s	5.7
'60s	5.1
'30s	2.4
Other Categories:	
Journalists and Critics	8.2
Oscars	5.4
Animals	1.6
Politics	1.4

Most-mentioned stars (not tallied under *Eras*, above):

Humphrey Bogart	2.6
Clark Gable	2.4

	Percentage
Topic	*of Questions*
W. C. Fields	2.1
Frank Sinatra	2.1
Marilyn Monroe	2.0
Bob Hope	1.9
Burt Reynolds	1.7
Charlie Chaplin	1.7
Judy Garland	1.6
Elizabeth Taylor	1.6
Paul Newman	1.6
Mae West	1.5
Richard Burton	1.4
James Dean	1.4
Ingrid Bergman	1.0
Bing Crosby	1.0
The Fonda Kids	1.0

On Screen (ON)

On Screen is one of the two most difficult categories in the Silver Screen Edition (Production being the other). ON, however, is far less intelligible than Production.

If you haven't gone to a lot of movies, don't go to ON: Even buffs will have a rocky time of it. This category often asks silly questions ranging from the brand of cleanser used by a character in *Close Encounters of the Third Kind* to the one line of dialogue cooed by Suzanne Somers in *American Graffiti*.

Nearly half the questions are of this ilk. What this means is that On Screen isn't exactly trivia, since trivia by definition gives experts a fighting chance; ON is drivel.

At least the nonsense is spread evenly across celluloid so *everybody* will be wiped out.

Diversity: ★★
Difficulty: ★★★★

Topic	Percentage of Questions
'60s Movies	17.7
'70s Movies	13.6
'30s Movies	10.0
'40s Movies	9.5
Nonsilent Comedy	8.1
'50s Movies	8.0
Westerns	5.1
Animated Cartoons	4.8
Science Fiction	4.6
War Films	4.3
James Bond	2.9
The Godfather	1.8
Musicals	1.6
Horror Films	1.5
'80s Movies	0.9
'20s Movies	0.8

Production (PRO)

Once more, merely going to the movies isn't going to help you with this category. You have to have read *People*, *American Film*, and a lot of history books.

Salaries, source novels, names of directors, film locations, and advertising (which, below, is included in the subcategories rather than broken out) are all a part of what the gamemakers call Production.

Only 10 percent of the questions can be considered unknowable in the same sense as those in On Screen; the rest represent a good, clean fight.

Diversity: ★★★★
Difficulty: ★★★★

	Percentage
Topic	*of Questions*
Stars Lives/Careers	9.7
'60s Movies	8.7
Directors/Producers	8.5
'70s Movies	7.6
'30s Movies	7.4
Technicians and Terms	6.3
'40s Movies	5.0
Science Fiction	4.6
Oscars	4.3
'50s Movies	4.2
War Films	4.0
Comedy	3.8
Animated Cartoons	3.8
Novels and Plays to Film (excluding *The Godfather* and *Jaws*)	3.2
Musicals	3.1
'20s Movies	2.3
Westerns	2.0
'80s Movies	1.4
Horror Films	1.3
James Bond	1.3
X-rated	0.6

Portrayals (POR)

This category is the human equivalent of SET but instead of wanting to know time and place, the authors ask who played whom.

Here, clearly, the buff has the edge; the novice has the same wing-and-a-prayer chance as in SET.

For the buff:

Diversity: ★★★
Difficulty: ★★

For the novice:

Diversity: ★★
Difficulty: ★★★★

Topic	Percentage of Questions
'60s Movies	24.7
'70s Movies	17.6
'40s Movies	11.3
'50s Movies	11.0
'30s Movies	8.4
Horror Films	4.7
Musicals	4.6
Oscars	3.8
Science Fiction	3.8
War Films	2.3
Westerns	1.3
Novels and Plays to Film	1.3
The Godfather	1.2
'80s Movies	0.9
TV Movies	0.4
Jaws	0.3
'20s Movies	0.3

How Many Times Are They Going to Ask This @#$% Question?

At least once during every game, players with a good memory will get a lucky break: They'll hear a question that is vaguely familiar. That's because up to 5 percent of the questions in every category of Trivial Pursuit are answers to other questions. As discussed in Part One, fielding these questions is *not* the same as taking one which you've had before. They're perfectly legal.

You may be wondering why there are redundant questions in the game. Isn't there enough trivia around to prevent such cases of *déjà vu*? Yes, but let's face it: To err is human. Some amount of cloning was bound to occur.

One example of the kind of recycling you can expect:

In the Portraits category of Silver Screen, one question is "What was the secret identity of Lawrence Talbot as played by Lon Chaney, Jr.?" and another is "Who played the title role in 1941's *The Wolf Man*?"

In two instances, the game actually asks the identical question twice. One Baby Boomer TV query is "What comedy anthology series made its debut on ABC in the fall of 1969?" while another is "What ABC comedy anthology series marked its debut in the fall of 1969?" The answer is the same for both. In a second instance, the same wording is used both times: "What actress was the highest-paid woman in the U.S. in 1935?" Fortunately for the game's credibility, the same answer is given both times.

Incidentally, these repeaters are one reason the game makers instruct players to return a card to the back of the deck once a question has been asked. It's a good rule. Many players hold on to cards to see if a different category comes up, which can be their undoing: Over 10 percent of the cards have two or more similar questions. For example, one Silver Screen card has three separate questions about *The Poseidon Adventure*.

Sometimes the Answer Is in the Question

Occasionally, the authors of Trivial Pursuit give players a push toward the answer. Comparatively speaking, there aren't a lot of these questions: Just under 10 percent of the questions tip their hands, so you've still got to know your trivia to win the game. But the clue questions *do* come in handy, provided you recognize them for what they are.

The hidden clues range from the obvious to the glib to the obtuse. The key to distilling these queries from the pack is to listen carefully to the wording of the questions, as the examples below will show.

Clue #1: Look for out-of-place language. You can bet you are being clued to the answer when a glaringly out-of-place word or phrase appears in a question. For example: "What NBC series would you believe debuted on 9/18/65?" (Baby Boomer TV). The giveaway is "would you believe."

Clue #2: Examine the question in more than one way. There are times when the answer is right before your nose; all you need do is look at the question in a new light. Example: "What happened on February 14, 1929?" (Genus Edition H). If you know anything about history, your impulse will be to shout, "The stock market crashed?" However, if you pause to listen to the date, you'll realize it's Valentine's Day—and this realization should give you the answer.

Clue #3: When is doubt, guess the question makers' favorites. After a while, players will become familiar with the favored watering holes of the game's creators. For instance, the detectives mentioned most by name in Trivial Pursuit are Sherlock Holmes, Charlie Chan, and Sam Spade. Holmes makes *seven times* as many appearances as the other two; thus, when a Genus AL question asks for the name of the detective who can distinguish between 140 forms of tobacco ash, he is the logical choice. JFK and Nixon likewise dominate the questions about U.S. presidents; *Playboy* rules the hutch where magazines are concerned; and *The Poseidon Adventure* is the correct answer to more questions about 1970s motion pictures than any other film. Watch for these pockets of favoritism: They could help you through a few trouble spots.

Clue #4: The answers are usually easier than you think they are. On the surface, some of the questions seem so impossible that your inclination is to wonder if the question makers are insane. Surprisingly, many of them are more swagger than substance. Though the game makers are not averse to throwing us a few wicked curves (see below), they are less sadistic than they could have been.

It isn't exactly Pythagorean, but this formula works in most cases: The more outrageous the question, the simpler the answer. For example, if the gamemaster asks, "How many grooves does one side of a 45-rpm record contain?" your inclination may be to babble, "*God* only knows! Eighty-two thousand? Seven million and two?" Of course, you realize that by taking scattershots like this you have a one-in-a-google chance of being right. So instead, you get a grip on yourself and ask if the authors of Trivial Pursuit are *really* showing off—or if they're merely displaying a puckish sense of humor by asking a question that *seems* complex but isn't. Could the answer be just the opposite of what it appears, something *simple*?

Since you can't get much simpler than one, you begin to wonder whether a record might not be made up of one groove, one continuous spiral. It makes sense.

Don't misunderstand: The questions *can* be brutal . . . but they aren't always.

Clue #5: The obvious is correct. When you find yourself totally baffled by a question, go with the obvious answer: More often than not, the apparent answer is right. For instance, if the question is "What was the name of the dog that played Toto in *The Wizard of Oz*?" don't guess "Spot," "Ruff," or "Athelstane." Look no further than the question for your answer. As for "What was the *Twilight Zone* called when it expanded from thirty to sixty minutes?" let common sense be your guide. (You should never guess *The Twilight Zone Hour*. Think: Shows that use "Hour" as part of their title are invariably variety programs or dramas where the sponsor's name is *also* part of the title, as in *The Alcoa Hour*.)

Not that Trivial Pursuit won't stick its tongue out at you now and then. Alas, the only protection against certain questions is encyclopedic knowledge or a very lucky guess. A question will read "What was the name of Isaac Newton's pet dog?" If you've grown accustomed to responding with the obvious, you will probably reply "Apple" or "Gravity." You would be wrong. Or a question will intentionally omit key information, as in the one that asks you to name the TV series which starred "six female impersonators during its seventeen-year run," implying that these impersonators are human beings. They're not.

Sometimes the game's authors will go so far as to ask an out-and-out trick question such as "Who's buried in Grant's Tomb?" When that Genus H irritant pops up, players wrestle with the Catch-22 of answering either "Grant and so-and-so" or sticking with the trusty old "Ulysses S. Grant." Most players opt for the latter thinking to avoid one of the oldest gags in recorded history. These same players sneer and curse when they learn that someone else is interred there as well.

Whatever type of question you face, if you have any doubt about the way it's been read, ask to see the card. While your opponent is not permitted to mislead you intentionally (at least not by gross misreadings; see Part Four on the psychology of the game), there are instances where this is unavoidable—especially when foreign words or expressions are involved. For instance, if you're asked to translate the Latin phrase which, phonetically, is "Uh-rah-ray yu-man-im," you may fare better reading it yourself. Seeing *Errare humanum* in type may suggest the answer, whereas hearing it pronounced will not.

The Lowdown on Incorrect Answers and Misleading Questions

Speaking of *Errare humanum*, the creators of Trivial Pursuit make out-and-out mistakes and also couch questions in language that is too vague for fair play. Although there are only about thirty-six wrong or misleading questions, and they are not a serious defect in the enjoyment of Trivial Pursuit, players should be aware of them. After all, at some point one of these questions might be a game winner.

Here are some of the errors to look for when playing the game:

1. The running time of *Gone with the Wind* is not 220 minutes. Sources from 1939 give the film

from two to five minutes more. (Silver screen PRO)

2. The authors also award *Gone with the Wind* one Oscar less than it actually won: The correct number is ten. (Genus E)

3. Peggy Lee did not provide the voice of Lady in *Lady and the Tramp*. Barbara Luddy did the honors; Ms. Lee gave voice to four *other* characters in the film. (Silver Screen PRO)

4. Joseph Cotten's first film was not *Citizen Kane* but *Too Much Johnson*, made two years before, in 1938. (Silver Screen PRO)

5. The unmade sequel to *Close Encounters of the Third Kind* was not *Close Encounters of the Fourth Kind*. It was *Night Skies*, which evolved into *E. T.* (Silver Screen PRO)

6. *Godzilla* was filmed in 1954 and released in the U.S. in 1956—not 1955. (Silver Screen PRO)

7. Julie Andrews did not land her role in *The Sound of Music* because of the success of *Mary Poppins*. The latter film hadn't been released when *The Sound of Music* went into production. (Silver Screen PRO)

8. Lois Lane didn't "yank off" Clark Kent's glasses to reveal his secret identity in *Superman II*. He removed the glasses himself to wipe away the spray from Niagara Falls. (Silver Screen ON)

9. Percival Lowell didn't discover the planet Pluto. The honor belongs to Clyde Tombaugh, who was working at the Lowell Observatory. (Genus SN)

10. Double Doody was not Howdy Doody's brother but the *first* version of Howdy. The substitution was made when the puppet's design became the object of litigation. The on-air explanation was that the character had undergone plastic surgery. (Genus E)

11. Only one brain was evil and "terrorized" earth-

lings in the movie *The Brain from Planet Arous*. The other alien was a benign police brain who wanted to capture the wanton cerebrum. (Baby Boomer SS)

12. Red kryptonite does indeed harm Superman. It isn't fatal, but it causes wild disruptions in his metabolism. (Baby Boomer PUB)

13. One and seventeen are *not* the only numbers which divide evenly into seventeen. They are the only *whole* numbers. Fractions are also numbers, meaning 8.5 is also correct. (Genus SN)

14. Mozart did not compose *Twinkle, Twinkle Little Star*; he wrote the music to which the words were added in 1806—fifteen years after his death. (Genus E)

There are also questions which are wrong *now*, though they were correct when composed:

1. Sean Connery's last performance as James Bond was in *Never Say Never Again*, not *Diamonds Are Forever*. (Silver Screen PRO)

2. The longest-running Broadway play is no longer *Grease* but *A Chorus Line*. (Genus E)

Then there are several questions that have two correct answers, such as:

1. Sgt. Schultz's "standard copout" on *Hogan's Heroes* is "I know nothing!"—invoked more often than the long form mentioned by the game's creators, "I see nothing, I know nothing!" (Genus E)

2. In *All That Jazz*, Joe Gideon said "It's showtime!" as often as he said "It's showtime, folks!" (Silver Screen ON)

3. *Annie Hall*'s Alvy Singer lived under the Cy-

clone—which is no less correct than "A Coney Island roller coaster." (Silver Screen SET)

4. When the authors of the questions ask which actor defended the Caine mutineers, they fail to specify Broadway or film. (Genus E)

5. Although Boris Karloff played the monster in *Abbott and Costello Meet Dr. Jekyll and Mr. Hyde*, Lou Costello and members of the London police force *also* became monsters. (Genus E)

6. The explorers in *Journey to the Center of the Earth* emerged into *two* seas: not just the Mediterranean, but also the Sargasso. (Silver Screen SET)

7. The question "What glaring addition was there in the remake of *The Thief of Bagdad*?" is doubly troublesome. The answer the game makers are looking for is "sound," though "color" is actually more accurate ("glaring" suggests visuals; "blaring" would have implied sound). Moreover, the question should have specified "*first* sequel," since there have been four versions in all. (Silver Screen PRO)

8. Ben-Hur used *two* standard pieces of equipment—not one—in the chariot race: the whip, as indicated on the card, and also a helmet. (Silver Screen ON)

Occasionally, the game makers pose questions that contain erroneous information. However, instances such as these don't alter the answer to the question, and the question should be played. A few examples are:

1. H. G. Wells' father was a shopkeeper, not a cricketer. (Genus AL)

2. Edgar Allan Poe's middle name is twice misspelled as Allen. (Genus AL)

3. The *Eye of the Needle* character was Die Nadel, not Die Nagel. (Genus E)

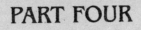

PART FOUR

PSYCHING OUT
YOUR OPPONENTS

Like most board games, Trivial Pursuit is supposed to be fun. And what could be more fun than psyching out your opponent?

Don't dismiss good-natured psychological warfare as *grossly* underhanded or unfair. There's nothing wrong with a sprinkling of psychology, nor should there be a stigma attached to a bluff here, a stone face there, a bit of intimidation somewhere else. Psychology helps to make you a total player, like an actor who brings more than just a good memory to a part.

As you have no doubt realized, most psychological tactics can only be worked when *you're* asking the questions. However, you shouldn't underestimate the amount of information you can glean from a reader by her or his inflection, as well as sighs and other sounds when the question is read. (Of course, you must make certain your opponents haven't studied this book.)

How to Force Your Opponent into a Wrong Answer

Too many good players make the mistake of approaching Trivial Pursuit with the kind of sobriety attached to playing cards. Wrong! Trivial Pursuit isn't poker: You're not trying to seduce the other player into upping the ante;

rather, you're attempting to keep him or her from thinking. In a game where an answer can suddenly come to a player, it helps your cause to make the person *feel* rushed even if she or he isn't.

To this end, pick the card quickly, but *do* pause long enough to read both the question and answer to yourself before turning to your opponent. (You especially want to read the answer to yourself when the question is easy—this is done to make your opponent believe the question is difficult.) Next, hurriedly read the question out loud and then immediately return the card to the box (so that your opponent will be reluctant to ask for the question again).

How to Use Your Voice to Trick Opponents

When reading the question aloud, you should endeavor to do so in as *College Bowl* a voice as possible. The more official you sound, the better.

Obviously, you can't go so far as to change the cadence of a question to mislead your opponent. An extreme example would be "Who was the first important *native* American novelist?"—the misplaced emphasis implying that the answer is Ruth Beebe Hill and not James Fenimore Cooper. But in a question such as "What was the nickname of Civil War general Thomas Jackson?" you'd be foolish to say, "...general Thomas *Jack*son." That's the emphasis most of us place on his nickname (*Stone*wall *Jack*son). The canny player hits hard on the "*gen*eral," after which the voice trails off. Likewise, when asking "Who used AuH2O as an election slogan?" don't pause between "Au" and "H2O." Read it "A-u-H-2-O," simply emphasizing each character equally—or even cheating a tad and running the A-u-H together.

If you're game, you can actually work wonders with the verbal feint. For example, if you smirk (as though to say, "Of *course!*") and in a slightly nasal, singsongy voice ask, "How much money did Jack Benny take home on *The $64,000 Question?*" (accenting "How," "money," and "Benny"), your opponent will probably jump at your lead, guessing either $64,000 or thirty-nine (the number most associated with Benny). Both of which are *wrong*.

Where quotes are involved, the same muddle-it-up rule applies, in the sense that you should avoid cliché readings. For example, there's little you can do if the question asks for the origins of "Quoth the raven 'Nevermore,'" since the answer is in the quote. However, with a phrase like "What hath God wrought?" you can emphasize the "hath." Someone who might have recognized a more traditional reading ("What" and "wrought" emphasized) may be thrown off. As the sage said of chicken soup, "It may not help, but it can't hoit."

Incidentally, many players mistakenly believe that a monotone will help to "conceal" clues and other key bits of information; in fact, a monotone does just the opposite. The more closely the other player has to listen, the more likely he or she is to *hear* those clues.

Making "Interesting" Editorial Comments

Editorial comments are most useful when you draw a moronically simple question such as "What is one plus one?" Approximately 15 percent of the questions in the game are almost that easy, and when you pick one your goal should be to make your opponent doubt the obvious.

No, you don't want to lie, and it would be extreme to gasp, "Jeez, you'll *never* get this," as though the answer "two" couldn't be more wrong. However, there's no reason you can't say half under your breath, "That's interesting!" or "I didn't know that!"—implying that the apparent answer isn't the correct one. You'll come up with your own favorite comment, but other misleading expressions for simple questions include "I don't believe that," "Where do they *find* such blather?" and "We may hafta look this up."

Conversely, if you pull a difficult question, a quiet "Of course!" or "This one's a cinch" is usually enough to make players think less deeply than they should.

As in a trial, however, more important than the opening remarks are the closing statements. This is particularly true if your opponent seems unsure of an answer. Few comments from the reader are more unsettling than "Are you *sure* you want to go with that?" or "Uh—is that your answer?" The object is to make your opponent think that you can't believe he or she said something so dumb and, further, that you have only his or her best interests in mind. Saved for a critical juncture and uttered with all the compassion you can muster, you can lead a player from a right answer to a wrong one.

Hurrying opponents along can also be accomplished by asking, "Do you want me to read the question again?" If they'd wanted that they would have asked. The effect of your concern will be to make them feel guilty for taking so much time.

If you're playing with a group of people and aren't the reader, don't sit mutely on the sidelines. If a player is wrestling with a stumper, turn to someone else and quietly pose a question that has nothing to do with the game—about the kids or about the '56 T-bird the person is rebuilding. The player whose turn it is won't function as well when no one seems to give a hoot about what she or he is doing. By indirectly blunting the person's sense of competition, you nudge him or her a step closer to throwing in the towel on a particular question. If your opponent protests (though most won't for fear of seeming like a sore sport), simply smile and say something deflective like "We didn't want to pressure you," or "We were just trying to stay awake." That'll keep the scene from turning ugly.

Whatever the situation, don't look upon any of this as unsporting. Trivial Pursuit is no mere game—it's a war!

Making Noises

These serve the same purpose as editorial comments, though they are less intrusive and can be used more frequently. A sigh or a moan can signal to your opponent that he should have *no trouble* getting *this* one, while an emphatic "*Oy!*" or ominous "Uh-oh" can take the place of "You'll never get this!"

Again, in both instances just the opposite is true.

Other helpful noises are a single laugh accompanied by a deliberate shaking of the head (suggesting obviousness and encouraging the player not to think things through), a satisfied snort (purely intimidating, as in "Have fun with *this* one, old shoe!"), and utter silence accompanied by a raised brow ("You may *think* you know the answer, but think again").

Whatever your sound or morpheme, keep in mind that its object is to get the other player to reconsider his or her first impression. With a little prompting, even seasoned players can be made to go from the right answer to the wrong one. Take it from the voice of bitter experience.

How to Distract Opponents by Fidgeting

There's a fine line between annoying another player and being cagey. You don't want to cross it, or you'll be enjoying a lot of solitaire Trivial Pursuit (see Part Five). Everything depends on how you finesse each situation.

If your turn is next and you want to edge a deliberating opponent toward craven submission, pick up and shake the die for a moment. Rest and then repeat, rattling it lightly. You can begin this immediately after the card is replaced, or wait a beat. The effect will be to call attention to the fact that you're waiting for your opponent to make his or her move.

Fidgeting with the cards is another good ploy. Jostle the box as though straightening its contents; check to see that you put the card at the end of the pile; make sure the last few cards are facing the right way. Remember: Your seeming apathy will hasten an opponent's surrender.

Whatever you do, try to make your restlessness game-oriented. Absently jiggling the ice in your drinking glass and folding and unfolding an hors d'oeuvre napkin are borderline tactics, and leaving the table is acceptable but self-defeating (implying that it's all right for your opponent to take more time with the question). *However*, toying with your watchband, drumming on the table, or whistling are overtly obnoxious and should be avoided.

What to Do When It's *Your* Turn to Answer a Question

If you're faced with a player who is up on all kinds of wicked ploys, your job is to discover whether the reader is shamming you. If he or she isn't, you can use many of his or her inadvertent revelations. If the questioner *is* shamming you, you must find ways to ignore his or her tricky devices.

Are you being had? If you're playing someone you know, seeing through the person's bluffs shouldn't be much of a problem. You'll know pretty much what to expect from those who are practical jokers. The difficulty arises when you have to face a new opponent.

The key to pigeonholing your opponent is to watch the person during the first few rounds. As a rule, the player who becomes vociferous and/or physical when he or she gets an answer wrong is not going to try to sham you. People like this are too emotional, too caught up in being challenged and too entertained by the questions to be calculating. The players to beware of are those who wear the calm, vaguely amused manner of James Bond in a casino. The kind of cool player you, yourself, are trying to be.

What if your opponent is trying to trick you? The surest way to undermine anything an opponent might try to do is to ignore the person. However, there's an art to this, and it starts with the instant you have spun the die. Don't look at the person when the question is read—there's no need to open yourself up to intimidation. At the same time, you don't want to seem nervous by glancing here and there, so just keep your eyes on your token, trying to imagine it one wedge fuller. Once the question has been read, pull the carpet out from under your opponent by asking to read the card. Place it before you on the table, floor, or bed and reread the question (thus undermining any effort the person has made to "reinterpret" it for you), then continue to stare at it while you work up your answer.

If you don't want to appear so formal, fearing that your strategic macho will put a damper on the proceedings, make your *own* distractions. Bow your head, putting your hands on your ears and drumming the back of your neck; clap or punch your open palm; growl in frustration—anything to make whatever someone else might try seem... well, trivial. Your self-respect may suffer, but at least your game will not. In fact, many players find primal outpourings helpful in cleansing the brain and clearing the byways to long-locked vaults of trivia.

Six Things Good Players Never Do

1. Don't sing. When the question involves a song title, never warble, whistle, or hum it. Someone who doesn't recognize *Some Enchanted Evening* as the title of a song from *South Pacific* may, however, recognize the melody.

2. Don't demonstrate. When posing a question such as "Who was known as the Sweater Girl?" don't cup your hands beneath your breasts. Before you started handing out hints, your opponent may have thought the answer had to do with perspiration.

3. *Don't impersonate*. When reading a question such as "Who was the host of *The Twentieth Century*?" don't affect Walter Cronkite's voice, irresistible though it may be when you're caught up in the spirit of the moment. The same holds true for actors, sportscasters, politicians, etc.

4. *Don't garnish*. "In what city does *Charade* take place?" shouldn't be read with a French accent.

5. *Don't editorialize in a helpful manner*. Apart from the feints, keep your jokes and personal opinions to yourself. "Which Kahlil Gibran book is his masterpiece?" should not be followed by "... and made him lots of profits."

6. *Don't query*. If the question is "Name the first black to play major league baseball," don't take it upon yourself to inquire if the game makers mean the Negro League or the National League. If the player doesn't know enough to request clarification, let him or her stew.

If properly handled, not only will these psychological ploys give you an edge, they'll add enormously to the challenge, depth, and satisfaction of playing Trivial Pursuit.

PART FIVE

NEW WAYS TO PLAY TRIVIAL PURSUIT™

It can be argued, persuasively, that part of the appeal of Trivial Pursuit is its simplicity. You answer a question, you keep going. You mess up, and someone else goes. After many months of playing the game in this manner, you may want to explore new ways of playing Trivial Pursuit.

What follow are games that suggest *alternatives* to the basic game of Trivial Pursuit. Many of these variations will be particularly enjoyed by players who may not know as much trivia as their regular opponents. Strategy and intelligence—as opposed to pure knowledge—are the factors that determine who will win.

(Note: None of these variations has been endorsed by the creators of Trivial Pursuit. They are presented solely for the amusement of the reader who wishes to expand the versatility of the basic game kit.)

Trivia Detour

This game is similar to the original Trivial Pursuit with one significant difference: Your token serves as a brick wall. Wherever it is, no one else can pass it. Nor can you move past another player's token.

The sole exception: If a player is on a regular colored

space surrounded on both sides, or on a headquarters surrounded on three, he or she can move after correctly answering *two* questions in that category. If the player can answer, he or she may roll and move out as though there were no impasse. If not, the player stays put and loses a turn.

The fun of Trivia Detour is being able to actually *control* sections of the board. Like a modern-day King Arthur, you're not only questioning, you're conquering—a rather exciting prospect for the megalomaniacs among us. A player who positions herself or himself on a spoke close to a headquarters can effectively block that headquarters from players approaching on any of the three sides. Or a player trying to get onto a headquarters can have the bad luck of rolling the right number to get there when someone else is already there—in which case that player must move *away* from the headquarters, possibly putting himself or herself out of one-roll striking distance.

Not only are the areas of supremacy constantly changing, but the more people there are playing Trivia Detour, the more exciting the game becomes. Consider: It's possible for a player to be on the hub, a spin of six from the last headquarters she or he needs, and be unable to get any *closer* than twenty-one spaces from that headquarters!

Trivia Dice

Players who must frequently face a superior foe lament that there is no such thing as a handicap in the game. Trivia Dice helps to compensate for that.

The weaker player is allowed to spin *two* dice per turn, and is able to use the figure from one, the other, or both of them. For example, spinning a one and a three, the player can either move one, three, or four spaces. Trivia Dice is one of the few board games in which spinning a double can actually *hurt* you.

This variation gives the weaker player a greater chance of reaching roll-again and favorite-category spaces. That evens up the odds somewhat, although answering the questions remains the most important aspect of the game.

Trivia Assault I

This is the game virtually without sanctuary: The roll-again spaces are ignored and skipped over. The rim is played as though there were twelve fewer segments. On the other hand, the hub (or center) is used as a roll-again space.

Note that Trivia Assault I does more than merely eliminate the dozen outside pitstops. It makes any headquarters a single spin of five from the two adjoining it, which radically alters gameplay. Case in point: From any headquarters, any other headquarters is within one-turn striking distance, assuming the player can roll a six, hit the hub, then toss a six in turn. Thus, the hub (or center) not only becomes a desirable place to be, it can be strategically invaluable at times!

Trivia Assault II

Instead of being ignored, the roll-again segments belong to the same category as the nearest headquarters. What this can do is to set up a fortress around each wedge. Assume you're playing Genus and your weak area is Sports & Leisure. In Trivia Assault II, the roll-again spaces close to the SL headquarters become SL spaces. Land on them and you must answer an SL question.

To draw an analogy, assaulting a headquarters in Trivia Assault II is like trying to go around a Monopoly board that is fully stocked with hotels. The best you can hope for is not to be hurt *too* bad.

Trivia Holiday

This game is the antithesis of the two Trivia Assault variations.

Each player is permitted to make any *one* category in the game his or her personal wild card. Whenever the player lands on that color, a question is posed from the player's favorite category.

Thus, suppose you are playing Genus Edition and despise the Geography category, but love Entertainment. You can make all the blue (Geography) spaces on the board serve as pink (Entertainment) spaces and need never answer a Geography question.

Trivia Blockade

The object of this game is to mark off spaces so that your opponents cannot use them. Because this game is considerably different from Trivial Pursuit or any of the other games above, the rules require additional elaboration.

1. Play as you would ordinary Trivial Pursuit until one player takes a wedge.
2. Each time you conquer a headquarters, instead of putting the wedge in your token, hold it to block other players ("block wedges") or to free yourself from a blockade ("free wedges").
   a. The block wedge is always placed on the *inside* wall of the colored spaces, free wedges on the outside. (This is done to keep track of them, since free wedges do *not* block other players from moving through the space.)
   b. No more than three wedges of *any* combination can be hoarded in your hand. If a player expects to take a fourth wedge in a roll or two, he or she would be wise to put a wedge down on the board as either a block wedge or a free wedge.
3. Once a block wedge has been placed, only you can pass through the space it is on. Everyone else must go around it, with the following exceptions:
   a. If you place a free wedge on the space, you can go through.
   b. If a headquarters is blocked, you can go to the headquarters *if* you toss the number exactly. If not, you must go back that number of spaces.

(Note: If your route backward is blocked, the "hub rule," rule 4 below, is put into effect.)

c. If you're out of free wedges and anticipate having to move either in a blockaded direction or onto a blocked space, before rolling you can "challenge" whoever put the wedge in your way. That player must then pose a question from the category of his or her choice. Should you answer it correctly, you may roll. If more than one wedge lies within the number you might roll, you must answer questions from each player who has placed a wedge in turn. Miss any question and you don't get to roll. Your turn ends before it has begun. (*Note 1*: These passes cannot be "saved." If you fall short of the wedge through which you won a temporary pass, you no longer have a pass. *Note 2*: If you need a five to land on a headquarters, and there are wedges on the spaces four and six away, you can take a chance challenging *only* the wedge on space four. However, if you throw a six and can only move to an occupied space, the hub rule, rule 4, is employed.)

4. If for some reason you cannot move—for example, you're trapped inside an arc whose two ends are suddenly shut off, and you roll a six—you must go to the hub, your turn ending. Using it as a wild-card spot, remain there until you can correctly answer a question of your choice, after which you may roll out.

5. No more than three wedges in *any* combination can be hoarded.

6. The player wins by placing all of his or her wedges on the board and returning to the hub, whereafter the rules are the same as for Trivial Pursuit.

Players who have spent some time running through Trivia Blockade have found that the markers are most effectively used *not* to barricade headquarters but to keep players from favorite categories, especially the triads (the identically colored spaces surrounding a headquarters). Indeed, one player can effectively monopolize a complete arc by placing markers on every other segment.

It also encourages that ever-enjoyable option of two players beating up on one via cooperatively divvying up the board.

You'll find that the options presented by Trivia Blockade create ever-changing, strategy-oriented gameplay. They also make for a *longer* game, because of the often tortuous routes dictated by the obstacles on the board as well as frequent challenges.

Trivia Exile

Once in a while, you'll take a wild guess on a question for which you have no answer—and get the answer right. Most of the time you won't. In a regulation game of Trivial Pursuit, the worst that happens then is that your turn ends.

Not so in Trivia Exile. As the name implies, if you miss an answer, you can find yourself taking a quick trip to somewhere you don't want to be.

1. Begin as you would in Trivial Pursuit.
2. The first time a player misses an answer—either by silence or guessing wrong—the player whose turn is next may answer the question or pass on it. If the player passes, the question dies and nothing changes. If the player fields it and answers cor-

rectly, he or she may send the previous player to any segment on the board. The player who did the banishing then takes his or her regular turn, as in Trivial Pursuit.

3. If the *second* player to tackle the question also misses, the question is dropped. (With two wrong answers already having been eliminated, it would not be fair for the next player to have a shot at it.) However, if the second player got the first question right and misses the second, *this* question can be taken by the next player.

4. The hub is a wild card, but the same rules of play apply.

Obviously, players must be cautious about what colored spaces they choose to land on: If they tend to be weak in an area in which the next player is strong, it's best to avoid the category.

The real fun starts when a player is only one wedge from victory. Watching someone who is so close to winning get booted into the nether reaches of the board is enough to give even the most hopeless also-ran the enthusiasm to continue.

Trivia Empire

In the tradition of Trivia Blockade, though grander by far, Trivia Empire is a two-player game in which you use your wedges to create "kingdoms" and rule the board.

1. Each player selects a headquarters to be her or his "castle." Wedges are placed only in the other four

headquarters, the color of the wedge correspond-
ing to the color of the headquarters.

2. As in Trivial Pursuit, the player moves by answering questions, and is awarded a wedge for
each conquered headquarters.

3. The object of this game is to enclose sections of
rim and spoke, a segment within your kingdom
serving as one end, a wedge as the other. A kingdom wedge is identified by placing it on the board
with the open side down. Obviously, your first
placement must use the castle headquarters as one
of its ends, since that is the only segment within
your empire when play commences.

4. You must put down a wedge as soon as it is won.

5. A stretch of kingdom cannot include or pass
through the hub. For example, a player can't claim
two spokes by using the hub as a joint.

6. A stretch of kingdom cannot claim even a single
segment belonging to another kingdom. The exception is spy segments, discussed below.

7. Each player can move freely through the other
player's kingdom.

8. Two of your six wedges are spies. These can
infiltrate your opponent's kingdom and be used
to stake claims therein. Spy wedges are placed
with the open side up, and are the last two wedges
played. See rule 10, below. If one player's kingdom sections intersect—that is, a spoke and a rim
section share a common segment—and if the point
of intersection suddenly falls within a region con-
trolled by spies, *only that intersecting space* is
discounted. The rest of the abutting section remains in the player's possession.

9. The game ends when one of the players has put
down four wedges and made it back to his or her
castle headquarters. At that point, the spy wedges

are put down in turn, starting with the player who has returned to his or her castle.

10. Before either player's turn, except in the spy mode, the player can "attack" one of the opponent's wedges. This is done by taking one question in both of the categories adjoining the wedge. (If a wedge is bordered by a roll-again space, the attacker need answer only one question.) If both are answered correctly, the wedge is returned to the headquarters whence it came and must be won again. If the player misses one of the questions, the turn is forfeited.

Players of Trivia Empire will quickly discover that, as in chess, there are different opening gambits and countermoves depending upon the respective location of the castle headquarters. For example, if the castles are situated directly across from each other, both players tend to put their first wedge on one of the triad legs of their opponent's castle. That brings a sizable twenty-one-segment chunk into the kingdom. When this happens, each opponent, in turn, will usually respond by attacking that wedge to free up those spaces. (For this reason, players try to choose headquarters bordered by triads in a category with which they feel comfortable.)

With three different castle-to-castle relationships possible, players will enjoy investigating all such opening ploys and responses.

Trivia Toss-up

One of the most painful aspects of Trivial Pursuit is knowing an answer and not being able to shout it to the world.

Now you can—literally.

Trivia Toss-up is a game for three or more players. The set-up is the same as in Trivial Pursuit, as is the object of collecting six wedges and returning to the hub. How players collect their wedges, however, is quite different.

1. When a player lands on a category, rather than *taking* that question, he or she reads it to the other players. Whoever is the first to shout the correct answer gets to go next. In the case of a tie, a high roll on the die decides the matter.
2. If no one answers the question correctly, the player who read it gets to throw the die again.
3. There are only two times a player answers the question in the category on which he or she landed:
   a. When the player has landed on a headquarters whose wedge he or she needs.
   b. When the player reaches the hub at the end of the game.

Since five players screaming out an answer at once can become deafening as well as confusing, it is suggested that you limit Trivia Toss-up to three or four players. Even so, you would be wise to play when no one's trying to sleep.

Trivia Solitaire

While it's true that someone with nothing better to do can put a token on the board and move it through its paces in a kind of unpressured Trivial Pursuit, that hardly satisfies the urge many of us feel to break out the board and actually play competitively.

Trivia Solitaire solves that problem by structuring solo play so that we have an opponent.

1. Set up the board as though you're playing for two.
2. The first time you roll, move *both* tokens the same number of spaces—to the same segment, if you wish.
3. Take a question for each token. Make sure you select a different *card* for each question. (As noted earlier in the text, many questions on the same card tend to elaborate on or echo others on that card.)
4. If you answered both questions correctly, spin and move the two tokens the same number of spaces— again, either in the same direction or along different routes. If you answered only one question correctly, the other token misses its turn.
5. The roll-again spaces are treated the same as in regular play.

You'll be surprised at the difference it makes in solitaire play having a "token" adversary as opposed to just moving your piece absently around the board.

Trivia Race I

This is the only game in which wedges are not used. The object is to be the first to take your token through ten laps of the rim. Answer correctly and you spin again.

All of the players start in the hub and move out along the same spoke. Completing ten laps, they must return to the hub via that same spoke, entering the hub on an exact count, staying put on the spoke if they toss a number higher than they need.

There's no going backward in this game. Whatever you spin, that's the number ahead you've got to move, and the question you must answer.

Trivia Race II

Identical to Trivia Race I, except that each token has a handicap: It loses a turn if it lands on a category of its own color.

Trivia Hop

This is the equivalent of a "quickie," a slam, bam, abbreviated game of Trivial Pursuit. It isn't your basic break-out-the-pretzels-and-get-comfy game, but what it lacks in deliberation it makes up for in concentrated energy!

The rules are the same as in Trivial Pursuit, except for the following:

1. Each player starts on the headquarters of the same color as the token he or she selects and answers a question before rolling. If he or she answers the question properly, a wedge is won.
2. There's a five-second limit to the answering of every question.
3. The players can choose not to roll and remain on headquarters if they miss any headquarters' question.
4. The hub is played as a roll-again space during the game. After the six wedges have been collected, players can enter with the exact number or *over*, and needn't leave it if they answer the last question incorrectly.

Apart from being a pleasant way of spending a half-hour, Trivia Hop is an excellent means of prepping yourself while waiting for friends to arrive for a "real" game of Trivial Pursuit!

Trivia Botticelli

If you have gone through all the questions in your boxes, you don't need to buy new boxes of questions or write your own questions—you can play Trivia Botticelli.

When a player lands on a category, a second player reads that player the *answer* to the question. The first player must then come up with the correct question, helped along by the "cold, getting warmer, getting hot" responses of the second player.

Here's an example of how it works.

Player #2: The answer is: Peter Sellers.

Player #1: Who played Inspector Clouseau?

Player #2: Cool.

Player #1: What British comic actor died of a massive heart attack?

Player #2: Colder.

Player #1: Who played three characters in *The Mouse that Roared*?

Player #2: Getting warmer.

Player #1: Who played three characters in *Dr. Strangelove*?

Player #2: Boiling!

Player #1: Who played Dr. Strangelove?

Player #2: Cooler.

Player #1: Who played President Muffley in *Dr. Strangelove*?

Player #2: You got it!

Scoring is kept on a separate piece of paper, with a

limit of twenty guesses as to the correct question. Whoever has the lowest score at the end of the game wins.

Players do *not* get to go again when they get a question right.

PART SIX

TRIVIA TOURNAMENTS

Whether you organize a trivia tournament as a fundraiser for nonprofit or civic organizations, or are looking to find the trivia champion of your block, fraternity, or city, tournament play is a wonderful sport. If the gamemaster is good and the participants psyched, gameplay can be exhausting, exciting, infuriating, and frequently savage.

The Charitable Tournament

There are many reasons for holding a public trivia game or tournament. The first and most common is to raise money for a charitable institution. This is as popular among first-time players as it is among old hands at trivia, because the players assume that everyone else is taking part to further the cause rather than to stomp a few egos into the ground. People are more willing to play a game when they know they won't be leaving behind pride, esteem, or gray hairs.

At a charity match, money can change hands in a variety of ways. Depending upon local laws, attendees have been known to:

1. bet on each player, like horses—complete with exactas.

2. pay a flat fee for admission to the tournament.
3. pay for the right to play the game itself. (If they win, they get to take home a color TV or some such item.)
4. pay to have one of their trivia questions read during the game. If the question stumps one of the players, that question is put in a bin and the person who wrote it becomes eligible for a prize drawing after the match or series.
5. be admitted for free, but have to answer a set of trivia questions during the match in order to get out. Each sheet of questions is different, and before being allowed to leave, the player must pay a set fee for each wrong answer.
6. sponsor different categories, anteing up each time the player correctly answers a question in their category.
7. buy spaces on a game board, paying out whenever a player is vanquished thereupon.

Whether Trivial Pursuit and its ilk can successfully challenge Bingo as *the* staple of the church/PTO/DAR/Hadassah fundraising functions will depend upon whether or not trivia can overcome the image many people have of it as the pursuit of the idle intelligentsia. To help dispel this notion, Part Nine of this book contains a selection of "club" questions specially designed to show that trivial pursuits can be enjoyed by everyone. Even if they don't partake in a game or two, club sponsors or affairs coordinators will realize from the entertainment value of the questions that trivia are not only fun but highly promotable.

CHARITABLE TOURNAMENTS: BOARD-STYLE

There are two ways a charitable trivia tournament can be played:

1. With an existing boardgame
2. With players seated on a stage, answering questions read by a moderator/gamemaster

There are advantages and disadvantages to both.

The drawback of using a game like Trivial Pursuit in public play is that not everyone will be able to see the board. Most VFW buildings and elementary school auditoriums just don't have the capacity to project a board onto a screen the way they do for chess championships.

If your organization or club can spare the $100 or so, the best way to work around this problem is to rent a color TV camera and a projection TV from a local video shop. This not only allows attendees to see the board in a large hall, but it lets the sponsors zero in on the perspiring faces and lip-gnawing of the players. This works wonders in terms of audience appeal, for it bestows on a small-town trivia match the look and feel of a prime-time sports event. And if the gamemaster sounds like Howard Cosell, so much the better (or worse, depending upon your point of view).

If the expense of a TV is prohibitive, the next best thing is to find a gamemaster with the gift of gab. She or he can do the play-by-play, which under ordinary circumstances would be considered distracting, but in a charity match will add to the fun—especially if the moderator can engage the players in pointed repartee.

Speaking of television, your local PBS station might

be interested in knowing that more and more of such stations around the nation are using games like Trivial Pursuit to attract donations during televised fundraising sessions. Prominent local figures are invited to come and play, and the heats last for the duration of the drive. Since betting is illegal in most places, broadcasters ask viewers to send contributions to each participant's "warchest"—funds which, if that player wins, are matched by local corporations, restaurants, car washes, trash collectors, and the like. The value of this setup is that the more games a favorite local celebrity wins, the more his or her supporters tend to pledge as the tournament progresses.

If a trivia game still seems too quiet to make for a compelling tournament, you can always try these flamboyant embellishments: Tag-Team Trivia, Fourth Down, and Musical Tokens. They may not have the class of the basic board games, but they sure are lively.

In *Tag-Team Trivia*, you're paired with a player you can fall back on. Whether the board is that of Trivial Pursuit or *Time* the Game™, you each operate on half the board. Unlike tag-team wrestling, you don't actually swat your partner: If you find yourself getting slaughtered, you simply move your token to the other hemisphere and your partner fields questions for a while. Or, faced with a difficult category on your side of the board, you pass the buck by moving to your partner's side.

Fourth Down is a game which, like Tag-Team Trivia, allows you to boot yourself out of a difficult question. Prior to beginning play, the players decide how many times they can "punt" a question—that is, change places on the board with another player, forcing her or him to answer your stumper.

Finally, *Musical Tokens* is simply a trivia version of musical chairs. There's no quest, no wedges or cards to acquire. Players simply move their tokens to the beat of the music and, when it stops, they must answer a question from the category on which they find themselves. A point is scored for each correct answer.

(By the way, these variations also work well at *home*. Use the brief descriptions above as the foundation for rules of your own.)

Of course, neither straightforward Trivial Pursuit or one of the variations need be an island. An ongoing tournament can consist of a series of all of these games, something like a trivial decathlon; it all depends on how elaborate one wants the tournament to be.

CHARITABLE TOURNAMENTS: PANEL-STYLE

In panel-style tournaments, people get up on a stage or behind a podium and simply field an emcee's questions. The benefit of this kind of play is that instead of *dominating* an evening, a trivia contest can be a featured part of a fair, barbecue, or wedding.

If you're staging a panel-type trivia contest, it's best to write your own questions rather than dip into the questions that come with your Trivial Pursuit game. Your questions will be of more interest locally, thus helping to sustain audience interest.

It's best to begin such a face-off with four or five panelists, since you're more liable to encounter a variety of entertaining personalities. If you have only two or three people taking part and one's a dud, the contest will fall flat. It could also go by so quickly there won't be a chance to bet on the outcome (see below).

The rules for conducting a trivia panel are simple:

1. Anywhere from five to seven categories of questions are collected.

2. A moderator reads the questions, quizzing each player from the same category.
3. If a player misses, the question dies. The next player goes, being asked a fresh question from the same category.
4. If a player answers correctly, the next player goes.
5. In order to get out of one category and into another, the player must correctly answer *two* questions from that category. The moderator keeps score.
6. The winner is the first to have correctly answered two questions in each of the half-dozen or so categories.

The beauty of this format, from the player's standpoint, is that as in Trivial Pursuit, someone can get an imposing lead and then bog down utterly in the final category. Players stuck on the first question of the first category have been known to overtake players who were trying to answer the last question in the final category!

You will need approximately thirty questions per player. If they really bog down in one category and the moderator runs out of questions, have them readdress the stumpers they missed on their first tilt.

Variations on the panel-type format include one that is closer to the traditional spelling bee. That is, there are no categories, just a potpourri of questions:

1. If a player misses the question, the next player gives it a try.
2. If the second player misses, the first player is spared.
3. If the second player *gets* the answer, however, the first player is eliminated.
4. Play continues until only one player is left standing.

The problem with this game is that the liveliest, most crowd-pleasing players are invariably the least serious intellects. They always seem to be eliminated early, leaving the more learned (read: boring) players to hold the audience rapt with musings about Ring Lardner's middle name, the chronic disease suffered by Marcel Proust, and the claim to fame of Brooklyn Dodger pitcher Van Lingle Mungo. (Useful answers, these: Wilmer, asthma, and he was pitching in New York when the *Hindenburg* passed over on its fatal rendezvous with a mooring tower in New Jersey.)

Another variation on this format is to have the question stay alive until someone gets it. In this instance, the only person who is eliminated is the one who went before the player who finally answered correctly.

In terms of fundraising, the panel setup can be lucrative in the sense that people who come to a carnival solely to ride the roller coaster or eat fried dough may be encouraged to stop and bet. This is most effectively and profitably done by letting people read the list of trivia questions and having them put money on individual questions. For example, if they bet a quarter on a question that eliminates a panelist, they win one kind of prize; if they put a dollar on the question, they win another. If the number of people who bet on each question is unlimited, a great deal of money can be collected.

The only real problem with public trivia matches is that now and then an enthusiastic onlooker will shout out an answer. This isn't so much a problem in a "fun" match as it is in a "championship" contest. In both cases, however, it's up to the player to admit whether or not he or she knew the answer or heard what was shouted. If there's still a doubt, the moderator can insist that a new question is read.

The Serious Tournament

The basic rules of Trivial Pursuit are used in serious tournaments. The only exception is that a noncompeting gamemaster should always read the questions and be present to settle any and all disputes. If players are putting in the time and effort to play a series of games, they deserve the benefit of an impartial judge and a straightforward reading of the questions.

Tournaments can be simple things, played among friends, or they can span the breadth of a college campus. You can contact other players by sending invitations, putting up bulletin-board notices, or running a small ad. The format of the tournament will depend entirely upon how many players sign up. If there are just two of you, a best-of-seven series is sufficient to even out the fortuitous and bad draws, the right and wrong tumbles of the die, the lucky guesses vs. those unaccountable fits of amnesia.

If there are three players, whoever is the first to lose two games is eliminated, after which the remaining players do a best-of-five series. Four players should play a round-robin tournament—six games in which everyone plays everyone else once (that is, three games per player). To continue, a player cannot lose two of those three games. If one player took three games (only one player can accomplish this), then that player is the champion. If two players won two games, they run through a three-game playoff.

A round-robin match is still possible with five or six players, but with seven or more it becomes confusing.

The best course then is simply to establish a ladder: If you win, you keep on playing.

Not to make you paranoid but, rather, to make sure you are pursued *only* on the game board, be aware of the fact that a familiar cardplaying racket is beginning to rear its head in the trivia-game field. People will post a notice about a game, inviting you to call for details. You'll do so, set something up, and on the night of the game find yourself intellectually superior to the two or three other players. At some point, however, one of your hosts will suggest that you start playing for money, maybe a $1 or $5 per question, and you'll agree, hoping to pick up some easy cash; all of a sudden your opponents will start answering every question they draw. Before you know it, the scam will have cost you a small bundle. The moral: If you're going to play for money, make sure you know and trust the people. (Trivia buffs take note: Charlton Heston made his screen debut playing just such a flimflam artist in the 1950 motion picture *Dark City*.)

Finally, if you are going to host a serious tournament, you should arrange for a trophy or blue ribbon to be awarded the winner. Even if the tournament is being played among friends, it's a good idea to give the top player a prize, as it makes everyone work harder at the questions and think faster.

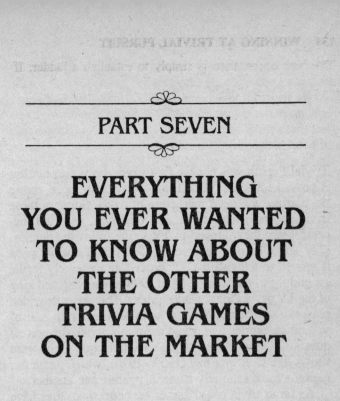

PART SEVEN

EVERYTHING YOU EVER WANTED TO KNOW ABOUT THE OTHER TRIVIA GAMES ON THE MARKET

Trivial Pursuit was not the first trivia showcase, nor has it proved to be the last. In the '40s, radio game shows popularized the mass marketing of trivia. Some of these trivia shows, such as *The $64 Question*, were so successful that they jumped to TV in the following decade. (*The $64 Question* became *The $64,000 Question* when it moved to television.) TV proved an extremely fertile ground for trivia; from 1964 to 1979, the undisputed king of the TV trivia shows was *Jeopardy*. This series provided players (and home viewers) with an answer in one of several categories and asked them to provide the correct question. On a somewhat higher intellectual plane were shows like *College Bowl* (1959–1970), which pitted our nation's most scholarly students against one another.

As far as trivia board games are concerned, they have boasted everything from the absurd to the sublime among their number. One of the finest board games—and one of the oldest—is Jeopardy™, which saw its fourteenth edition released in 1982.

Jeopardy™

There are over 2,300 questions in each Jeopardy™ set. Dollar per dollar, the game is the best buy on the market.

The game is played with answer sheets placed in a box and covered with a plastic window. (Remember: The player is given the *answers* and must respond with the questions.) Dollar markers are slipped into slots in the window, hiding each answer. The higher the dollar amount, the tougher it is to guess the question to the answer.

Looking quickly at a sample board, we find the categories Medicine, For Children Only, American History, 4-Letter Words, and Colleges. Selecting American History for $20, we read the answer "He was the first President of all fifty states." The gamemaster or emcee has a question book: When we give our reply, he or she checks to see if we were right. If we had been able to ask the question "Who is Dwight Eisenhower?", we would take a $20 bill from the stack of Jeopardy™ money. If for some insane reason we had asked some other question—such as "Who is George Washington?"—we would have surrendered that amount of money. When someone asks an incorrect question, the other players can snap their hand-held "cricket" noisemakers and try to guess the correct question.

The beauty of Jeopardy™ is that there are nearly fifty different categories per set, ranging from Sweets to Famous Pairs to Fictional Detectives. And while most of the information deals with popular objects, it's all surprisingly challenging. For instance:

1. The word means "omelet" to a Spaniard. (What is a "tortilla"?)
2. The pair of seas connected by the Suez Canal. (What are the Mediterranean and the Red Sea?)
3. He made his TV debut with dancer Barrie Chase. (Who is Fred Astaire?)

While the very straightforward, no-strategy-necessary play will leave some people cold, Jeopardy™ remains a lot of fun.

Time the Game™

Time the Game™, as one might expect, is the most sophisticated of all the trivia games. For one thing, the package itself is quite literary. There are no cards: The 8,000 questions (2,000 more than in Trivial Pursuit) are in four magazines, which are designed and sized like issues of *Time*. Each of the two, three, or four players gets one magazine; each magazine is different. The questions are true/false (worth ten points each), multiple choice (twenty points), and short answers (thirty points). Five hundred of the questions are for children.

The game also includes decade cards and point cards.

Time the Game™ is played on a square board consisting of thirty-eight segments. Most of these segments are labeled with a decade (1920s through 1980s) and a pair of categories. You must select a question from one of the categories and answer it. The categories are always grouped:

1. People/Places
2. Events/Arts
3. Sports/World

Somewhere on the board, every topic is paired once to every decade. Additionally, there are six segments of the board that have only one category on them. When you land on one of these, you get to pick the decade from which the question will be asked.

Finally, the four corner segments are reward or danger zones. The danger zones freeze players until they toss a certain number on the dice or surrender hard-earned points; the reward zones give players free choice of category *and* decade and let them go again.

On each turn, the player rolls three dice. The two white dice determine how many spaces one moves; the red die indicates whether the player is asked a ten-, twenty-, or thirty-point question. A roll of doubles on the white dice gives the player another turn.

The decade cards are handed to players the first time they land on a particular decade. When a total of sixty points have been achieved in any given decade, that particular decade's card is turned face-down. Thereafter, if a player lands on a segment for that decade, the player can ask for a question from any decade in which he or she doesn't yet have a full complement of points.

Points are tallied with point "cards," which look like Monopoly™ money. The points are handed out after each question is correctly answered and are placed beneath the appropriate decade card.

The player who is the first to win sixty points in each of the seven decades is the winner.

Questionwise, *Time* the Game™ is by and large more difficult than Trivial Pursuit. Part of this is due to the fact that unlike Trivial Pursuit, *Time* the Game™, has more questions from the 1920s and 1930s. That's fine for players who are sixty-five to seventy-five years old; otherwise, such questions represent a Little Shop of Horrors.

Even the multiple-choice questions from the 1920s and 1930s (and some from later eras) are unmerciful. For instance, if you weren't there and didn't read it in *Time* back in 1925, would *you* know whether it was a flood, earthquake, or tornado that killed 689 people in Missouri, Illinois, and Indiana on March 18 of that year? In this case, a blind guess would do more good than reflection:

We seldom think of a single tornado twisting through three states and would probably have guessed earthquake, then flood. But a tornado it was. Likewise, only a Calvin Coolidge booster or someone with the dumbest of luck would know that the President was sworn in *not* in Washington or Massachusetts, but in Vermont.

Most of the true/false questions are equally tough, though at least the odds of getting a correct answer rise to 50 percent from 30. As the following questions indicate, logic and education will have little to do with getting answers right:

1. The fiftieth anniversary of the electric light bulb was celebrated by Thomas Edison in Menlo Park, N.J. (true or false)
2. A popular dance from the 1920s, the Maxixe, came from Brazil. (true or false)
3. Broadway star Ruth Chatteron was a failure in silent films, though she later became the "First Lady of the Cinema." (true or false)
4. The first song to sell more than a million copies in sheet music was *What'll I Do*. (true or false)

In case you missed one or two, the answers are: (1) false (Henry Ford hosted the fête, so it was held in Dearborn, Michigan); (2) true (you might have fared better if the authors had provided its *current* name, which is the samba); (3) true; and (4) true.

The questions in the short-answer section aren't much easier:

1. Florenz Ziegfeld produced the *Follies*; who produced the *Scandals*?
2. Of what country was Eduard Benes the Foreign Minister?

3. This town was the Middletown of Helen and Robert S. Lynd's 1929 sociological survey.
4. What major political office was held by Lord Curzon in 1923?

The answers, for the record, are: (1) George White; (2) Czechoslovakia; (3) Muncie, Indiana; and (4) British Foreign Secretary.

When the question is set close to the present, the answer is more likely to come to you, but, unlike Trivial Pursuit, *Time* the Game™ doesn't offer many clues.

The one consistent failing of *Time* the Game™ is that the questions lack sparkle and personality. One is hard pressed to find a single question written with a hint or sense of humor.

Depending upon how much they like to be hassled by the *wording* of questions, players will either object to or enjoy the challenge of the many questions in this game that contain deliberately misleading information. In other words, while you're fighting to figure out the answer, you're unaware that a piece of erroneous information in the question has automatically rendered one answer wrong. Consider the following true/false questions:

1. The onetime Dutch colony Belize was granted its independence in 1981. (While you're busy sifting through the nethermost reaches of your mind to recall specifics about imperialism in 1981, the answer is "false" simply because Belize was a *British* colony, not Dutch.)
2. Oregon's Mt. St. Helens became active in 1980. (Once again, the date may be right, but the volcano is in Washington.)
3. Ian McKellen's performance in the title role of *Amadeus* won him a Tony Award. (This one's especially nasty since McKellen *did* win a Tony for

the play—though for his portrayal of Salieri, not Mozart.)

Approximately 6 percent of the questions in the game are of this type, which helps to make the game more difficult than it otherwise would have been. Again, this is not necessarily a *drawback*, merely an important difference between this game and Trivial Pursuit.

A much more comforting difference between the two is the fact that since all the questions and answers were culled directly from the pages of *Time*, the game is virtually error-free. There *are* a few items scattered about which might cause some semantic debate. For instance, after asking if *Amos 'n' Andy* was derived from a Broadeay show, the authors tell us that the answer is "false, it was spun off from a vaudeville act." The distinction between Broadway and vaudeville, while real in the strictest sense, is arguable in terms of the vernacular. However, contestable questions such as these are few and far between.

In the final analysis, it must be said that if *Time* the Game™ isn't as frivolously entertaining as Trivial Pursuit, it's a worthy opponent for those who have a nasty habit of breezing through trivia contests. In its stately way, *Time* the Game™ is in a class by itself.

A final word of commendation to the creators of *Time* the Game™. The use of old *Time* covers to illustrate the text *does* tend to bring each era vividly to life—certainly more so than the text alone would. More important, in the true/false questions, the correct answer to a "false" question is always "false"; but in some cases when the answer is "true" the game maker provides additional information. Although the player is not required to supply this material to win points, it's nice to know the data are all there. If nothing else, it makes *Time* the Game™ a more educational game by far than any of its competitors.

One final nice touch to *Time* the Game™ is that children's questions are provided. However, they aren't easy questions; indeed, many adults get fewer than half of them right. Don't believe it? See how you score on these true/false questions:

1. Dick Tracy's girlfriend is named Bess.
2. An Italian team won the World Cup in soccer in 1982.
3. Pele is a soccer player from Argentina.
4. The first President to speak on television was Harry Truman.

The answers are: (1) false (her name was Tess); (2) true; (3) false (he's from Brazil); and (4) false (it was FDR). And those are the *beginner* questions. The advanced section wants to know things like who invented Technicolor, where in the United States marijuana is legal, and whether Mr. Stouffer or Mr. Birdseye developed the process of fast-freezing vegetables.

If your children are young teenagers or have an IQ like a phone number, they may have a chance. Otherwise, plop your kids in front of the TV and play *Time* the Game™ with grownups.

Trivia Adventure™

Those of us who have been brutalized by hard-as-nails trivia questions in Trivial Pursuit and *Time* the Game™ can restore some of our sullied self-image by playing the children's game, Trivia Adventure™. Just flip through the cards and you'll find such soothing questions as:

1. What do we call a person who cuts down trees for a living?
2. What is a spider monkey: a spider or a monkey?
3. What is the opposite of "long"?
4. True or false: snakes shed their skin.

Obviously, Trivia Adventure™ is very different from the children's edition of the *Time* game. It's also more appealing in terms of its design aesthetics. However, Trivia Adventure™ has one serious drawback: too many editorial blunders and too much misinformation. More on this in a moment.

The board is a large, brightly drawn picture of the solar system's outer planets as well as a previously unknown world called "Quizzar." The object of the game is for players to proceed from Earth along a spiral path to the other worlds and finally to Quizzar. The first player to reach this planet is the winner.

Before the game begins, players must decide whether they will be answering the "A" (easy) or "B" (more difficult) questions. Two of each are printed on the game cards. Movement along the triangular spaces is determined by the toss of one die.

While traveling on these spaces between the worlds—each path ranging from a string of twenty-five to forty-six spaces—players answer questions from one of the 260 General Knowledge cards. A wrong answer is rewarded by a move backward of three spaces; a right answer allows a player to stay put until his or her next turn.

When players land on planets—either by throwing the exact number needed or a higher one—they must deal with questions from one of the 240 cards in the Special

Category batch. Each planet is assigned its own category as follows:

1. Mars: Storybooks and Fairytales
2. Jupiter: Heroes and Villains
3. Saturn: Cartoons and TV
4. Uranus: Language Arts
5. Neptune: Animals
6. Pluto: Games and Sports

If a player misses a question on a planet, he or she must once again retreat three spaces.

Upon answering a Special Category question correctly, the player is given a Collector Card. When the sixth of these has been collected on Pluto, the player must answer a General Knowledge question and hop to Quizzar. (If a player misses the Special Category question on Pluto, he or she does not move back three spaces.) The first player to make the complete trip from Earth to Quizzar is the victor.

Trivia Adventure™ is, of course, extremely entertaining for children ages seven and up. However, as mentioned above, it has many inaccuracies.

On the one hand, a good deal of confusion arises from the way questions are worded. One well-intentioned six-year-old when asked the General Knowledge question "Who do you call when you have a bad cold?" brightened and said, "My mom." Who would dare call him wrong, even when "the Doctor" is the required answer? Another child, age seven, asked to provide the name for a mountain of sand, replied "An ant hill" instead of a dune. Since both are *mounds* of sand, not mountains, neither is completely correct and the question was pitched. Yet another seven-year-old was asked the question "What was Chitty Chitty Bang Bang?" He answered, "A movie." That it was, though the answer the authors wanted was

"A car." However, the best answer any child has given to a Trivia Adventure™ question has to be this one: When asked "How did animals board Noah's ark?" the six-year-old replied *not* "Two by two" but "They used the ramp."

In short, too many of the questions are vague. They're also haphazardly punctuated, i.e., "Name the football teams based in New York?" (sic) Even worse than this, particularly in a game in which children are reading the questions, is the endless parade of misspellings. To name just a few, the authors have "nickles" instead of "nickels," "Muskateers" for "Musketeers," "Rupunsel" in lieu of "Rapunzel," "Bob Cratchett" instead of "Bob Cratchit," "Gramaphone" for "Gramophone," "kimo sabi" instead of "kemo sabe," and "Theodor Seuss Geisal" instead of "Theodore Seuss Geisel." One gets the uneasy feeling that there was more than a printer's gremlin at work here—that whenever they weren't sure of a correct spelling, the game's creators simply sounded out the answers and let it go at that.

Despite these incredible blunders, the *pièce de résistance* has to be the answer to the question "Who was the first American in space?" The authors say "John Glenn" instead of "Alan Shepard"—something so well known and so easily checked that it casts a pall of suspicion over everything else in the game.

If an adult plays Trivia Adventure™, reading all the questions and umpiring the answers, the game can be a worthwhile experience. Otherwise, keep away from it; just sit tight and wait for the Trivial Pursuit children's edition, challenge your kids with the young people's questions in this book, or write your own.

Other Trivia Games

Three new trivia games have been released in 1984. One is a game put out by *Ripley's Believe It or Not*®, another is one endorsed by *TV Guide*, and the third is a game endorsed by *People*. Of them all, *People* Weekly: The Trivia Game with Personality™ seems to have the best shot at achieving anything near the popularity of Trivial Pursuit. Not only does it have the name of the magazine behind it, but players who have no interest in the Tube category (an obvious drawback of the *TV Guide* game) can pick questions from Pages, Screen, Jocks, Chatter, and Song.

Structurally speaking, the *People* questions are actually more versatile than those in Trivial Pursuit, since they don't compulsively begin with Who-What-Which, etc. They do, however, reflect the glibness that trivialists have come to expect from these games: for example, "Name the Broadway show that has high-stepped its way into becoming the longest-running musical in history." (*A Chorus Line*, in case you missed it earlier in our text or the "high-stepped" clue eluded you.)

The Ripley's game is more a variation of TV's *Hollywood Squares* than Trivial Pursuit, since the players have to read what's written on a card or create a bit of incredible information in the Ripley's vein, and the other players have to guess whether the player made up the information or if it's "real" (i.e., "Highway 22 in Long Island is *haunted*! Cars which stop at a certain spot are burned by the ghosts of Indians and settlers *still fighting for control of the land*!"). Not very cerebral. . . .

Another new game, Family Trivia™, was announced shortly before this book went to press. As described, Family Trivia™ will be played on a board using questions actually written by family members for each other, such as "What kind of car does Sally's boyfriend drive?"; "Who is the oldest of Daddy's nephews?"; "Name the hospital in which mommy was born"; and so forth. The write-your-own nature of this game may go a long way toward eliminating the problems inherent in the other trivia games—that is, running out of questions and the impersonal nature of the topics. We shall see.

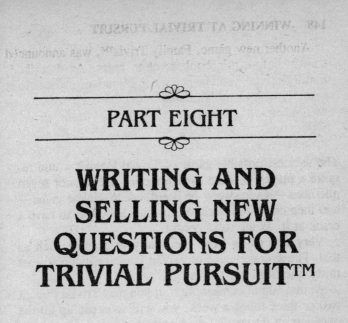

PART EIGHT

WRITING AND SELLING NEW QUESTIONS FOR TRIVIAL PURSUIT™

The shortest possible game of Trivial Pursuit would require a player to make twelve moves and answer seven questions—six to sweep the board, one to win the game—and then one more question for the challenger to have a crack at it, as the rules permit.

Very few of us have been party to a game such as that. The average game of Trivial Pursuit eats up at least thirty questions per player.

At that rate of consumption, if you play Trivial Pursuit two or three times a week, you will soon use up all the question on the cards. Your options, then, are to go out and buy new boxes of questions or write your own. While buying new questions is easy, it's a lot more expensive than writing your own—and not half as much fun. In addition, writing your own questions allows you to personalize the game. After all, the makers of Trivial Pursuit don't know your friends and family, and so can't ask: "How many times did Louisa have to propose to Charlie before he agreed to marry her?"

Most of us read a newspaper or watch the nightly news. The news is a source of great trivial riches. And not obscure trivia, such as the name of Don Quixote's horse (Rozinante).

News and entertainment trivia are, moveover, the *créme de la créme* of trivia, because they contain information to which most of us have been exposed. As we noted earlier, it's the tip-of-the-tongue kind of trivia question that makes us wrack our brains and reproach ourselves: If only we'd paid closer attention, we'd have the answers!

If you're creating questions with certain people in mind, this method also allows you to dwell on subjects you feel would add to their enjoyment of the game. There's no reason to stick to the categories used in Trivial Pursuit sets; you can go so far as to assign a color to "Last Month's Romance Novels" or "The Gospel According to Mark" if you so desire.

Writing your own questions, you'll find there's everything to gain, nothing to lose—and best of all, the questions are free!

The Seven Types of Trivia Questions

Be aware of the fact that every one of the questions composed by the manufacturers of Trivial Pursuit are cut from the same *structural* cloth. Each begins with Who (or Whose), What, How, Where, or When. While there are a few multiple-choice questions in each edition they, too, are presented this way. (For instance, All-Star Sports BKB offers the following multiple choice: "Which of Ernie DiGregorio, Calvin Murphy and Slick Watts hasn't led the NBA in assists?") Only true/false questions are worded differently. These are written so that the answer is "yes" or "no." (For example, BBL asks: "Can a pitcher get credit for a victory if he doesn't throw a single pitch?")

Within this framework, the questions written for Trivial Pursuit come in seven different varieties:

1. Questions People Think They Should Be Able to Answer... but Can't

Into this category go those questions whose answers we know but just can't jar loose or which seem obvious after-the-fact, such as the name of the song played before the Kentucky Derby or the name of the person who said, "Honey, I forgot to duck."

2. Super-Trivial Questions

There are questions even the subject mavens have trouble with, such as identifying the college at which *Breaking Away* was shot, naming Sky King's nephew, or describing the winning entry in the 1969 Pillsbury Bake-off.

3. Commonplace Questions Everyone Knows and Can Answer

Into this category fall questions such as the name of the man who killed Alexander Hamilton in a duel, the term which describes the front cutting teeth, or the title of the first book in the Old Testament.

4. Amusing Questions

Whether they're simple or difficult, these exist primarily to entertain the listener. For example, "Who told the cinematographer of *Sunset Boulevard*, 'Johnny, keep it out of focus. I want to win the foreign picture award'?" The *real* question, of course, is "Who directed *Sunset Boulevard*?"—but it's couched this way so we can enjoy Billy Wilder's wonderful quote.

5. Misleading Questions

These are queries which, by their wording, point you in one direction when the answer is in another. To wit: "What game is deadly to players over twenty-one?" Your mind starts ferreting through sports where bones are easily broken, then hops to the science fiction firmament, where you vaguely remember that age and/or athletics were the subjects of movies like *Rollerball* and *Logan's Run*. Through it all, you fail to realize that the authors aren't looking for an age but a card tally.

6. Fifty-Fifty Questions

In one of these there are only two or three probable answers, but you have no idea which one is correct. For example, asked to identify the world's largest chemical company, you know it's probably either Dow or DuPont. So you mentally flip a coin—invariably guessing Dow when DuPont is the right answer.

7. Trick Questions

These questions are intended to force you to offer idiotic answers. Two examples: "What star is closest to the earth?" and "What was the name of the airplane flown by the Wright Brothers?" Most of us hear "star" and sputter out something like Proxima Centauri or Sirius instead of the right answer, which is right under our nose (or tanning it, as the case may be); while as soon as "Wright Brothers" is mentioned, a surprising number of players automatically shout "Kitty Hawk!"—which is foolish, since that's where the flight took place. (Not that having bitten our tongues would have helped, since most of us don't know the correct answer.)

In Trivial Pursuit, the questions are more or less equally distributed throughout these seven categories. However, as a prelude to writing the questions, be aware of the fact that the pitfall into which many first-time question writers tend to stumble is favoring one style over another. More on this problem is our section on writing the questions.

How to Collect Material for Questions

If you have ever asked yourself what the heck can you do with your personal computer, you finally have your answer: You can use it to write and disseminate Trivial Pursuit questions. Computers are an ideal place to store your questions, not only in terms of organization and accessibility, but because many systems have a "lock" capacity on the file itself. The lock will keep your spouse, friends, siblings, or whoever from accidentally stumbling onto your answers while recording their *own* questions. Best of all, with a computer you can print out hard copy of the questions for as many friends as you can con into writing questions for *you*.

Naturally, a good old spiral notebook or index cards will give you the same results, albeit less efficiently than a computer. What's really important is that you have a good time collecting the material. You shouldn't write the questions right away—it's better just to amass trivia items and see what they look like, since certain topics are better suited than others to questions which are misleading, punning, amusing, and so on.

You'll be surprised to find that gathering trivia doesn't take long. If you're watching TV, you can do it during the commercials (you can even *use* the commercials as questions, e.g., "Which fast-food company knows where he beef is located?") If you're reading a newspaper or magazine such as *Newsweek* or *People*, jotting down notes can become second nature. You can even put asterisks in the margins of the paper or magazine if the person for whom you're writing the questions won't be reading that particular journal. (This earmarking and returning to information has the benefit of increasing your own retention, allowing you to impress friends by correctly spelling "Konstantin Chernenko" or identifying the Pacific and the Caribbean as the two bodies of water which border Grenada.)

You can also ask youngsters to lend a hand as they read *their* magazines, from *Videogaming Illustrated* to *Superman*. (They may provide you with real brain-twisters like "What was the first videogame to have a sequel?" and "What were the names of Lois Lane's parents?")

To illustrate the ease with which trivia questions can be assembled, the following ten questions were put together with material culled from just the first eight pages of a small-town newspaper.

1. What have Soviet scientists described as having a "tremendously harmful psychic effect" on young people?
2. What is the name of the Lebanese faction warring against the Christian Phalangists?
3. What professional device was used for the first time in college basketball during the 1983–84 season?
4. Whom did Johnny Carson agree to stop kidding in his monologue because too many prospective jurors admitted that Carson's quips had biased them?
5. On whose thirtieth birthday did her mother say, "Her quiet survival for eight years symbolizes the right to make your own decisions about your life"?

6. What TV actor became one of Hollywood's most in-demand directors because of the success of *Splash*?

7. What common compound mixes with water to cause carbonic acid—aka acid rain?

8. What did the West German military say helps teach potential soldiers "to be able to set off explosives and destroy the enemies of our free society"?

9. What did the Soviet Union say *really* caused the yellow color of the rain near their chemical-warfare plant in the jungles of Vietnam?

10. What is the second-largest city in Hawaii?

These questions took approximately ten minutes to scribble down in raw form, another few minutes to polish. Thus, an investment of just over an hour scattered through the course of a week can actually see a couple through an average game. And if you swap questions with friends and neighbors, you'll never again have to play Trivial Pursuit with questions you have had before.

(By the way, the answers to the questions above are: (1) rock and roll; (2) Druse Moslems; (3) the shot clock; (4) John De Lorean; (5) Karen Ann Quinlan; (6) Ron Howard; (7) carbon dioxide; (8) prime-time television; (9) the excrement of honeybees; and (10) Hilo.)

How to Create Your Own Categories

Don't think in terms of categories right away—wait until you have about twenty pieces of trivia. By that time you'll be able to see where the strengths, weaknesses, and similarities of your trivia lie. Otherwise, you'll find yourself trying to dredge up information just to *fill* the categories you picked, something which can be time-consuming or will dilute the final results. For example, if you were to come up with a question such as "What political book did Jimmy Carter publish prior to his election as President?" you might be wiser to put it in a category about the White House rather than trying to stock a category consisting solely of questions about contemporary non-fiction. (Of course, you could also put such a question in the category of humor—depending upon your political bent—since the answer is *Why Not the Best*?) Before you decide, wait and see what other questions there are to fill potential categories.

Once you have your six categories, start up a seventh called Miscellaneous. This serves two purposes: It can be a category you use during gameplay, or else it can be a warehouse of material to use at some later date. (The cardinal rule of writing questions for Trivial Pursuit is that *nothing good gets thrown away*.)

How to Write
Terrific Questions

When you have set up your categories, start putting the information into question form. Remember to vary the types of questions you ask. Your personality will lead you to favor certain kinds of questions: Punsters tend to write misleading questions; the cynical among us come up with super-trivial stumpers; while intellectuals usually take the time to whip up questions people think they can answer but can't—just to watch opponents squirm when they spring the answers.

The danger of giving in to what comes naturally is that if you play against people who know you, or if you meet the same opponents over and over, you're going to become predictable. Your adversaries will be looking harder at each question for your trademark and, finding it, will use their knowledge of you to help unravel the question. For this reason, it's recommended that before you write your questions, you read through a small stack of Trivial Pursuit cards and assimilate the variety of style. Osmosis really works, and it will show in the finished product.

Whatever style you use, the question should usually run no longer than twenty words. Although Trivial Pursuit questions use as many as twenty-four words, long questions invariably need to be repeated and tend to slow the game down, and they rule out some of the psychological strategies you can use. Just because you're writing the questions, don't forget that the tactics we've discussed for Trivial Pursuit still apply—within reason. You don't want to concoct a question such as "Who is the finest human being on this planet?" Your opponent can't be expected to know that the answer is *you*.

Also keep in mind that you must use precise language when writing questions. Here's an example. You're a stamp collector and you want to ask something about the hobby that's accessible but challenging. You decide to pose a question about recent increases in first-class postage. Depending upon your disposition, there are several ways you can ask the question.

The simplest and most direct way is "What were the last three rates for first-class postage before it went to twenty cents?" The answer is thirteen, fifteen, and eighteen cents.

However, if you wanted to make the other player "kneejerk" into the wrong answer, you might ask, "What were the last three increases in first-class postage?" Your opponent is likely to answer, "Fifteen to eighteen to twenty cents," which would be wrong, since the last three *increases* were two, three, and two cents.

Finally, if you only wanted to be mildly circuitous without compromising the essence of the question, you could ask, "How much less than the one before it was the most recent increase in first class postage?" The answer, of course, is one cent.

Naturally, if you knew your opponent to be a mathematical bungler, you *might* ask for the *sum* of the four most recent rates for first-class postage; playing a wizard, you could request the square root of the sum. That would not only demand that the player know the trivia, but that he or she do some mental athletics to boot. (More on complex questions such as these in the section on mindbenders.)

We've seen how the authors of Trivial Pursuit hint at answers using singularly revealing adjectives or turns of phrase. While clues are fun to work into questions, and can be used after the fact to needle players who don't pick up on them, most players resent the advantage hints give opponents. Thus, you're unlikely to toss a lot of clues into your own questions. At the same time, however, you don't want to produce a batch of questions so dry that they crackle when you hold the paper.

To make questions sparkle without relying on those jaunty clues, try to explore an oddball or interesting facet in a given item. Some subjects, such as politics, don't lend themselves to this, which is fine: Not *every* question has to be a ribtickler or raise eyebrows. However, if a subject can go either way, opt for the more entertaining and/or informative question. For example, don't ask, "Who played Lawrence of Arabia in the 1962 film?" That's needlessly dull and straightforward. Better to ask, "Who was Oscar-nominated for his portrayal of Lawrence of Arabia?" or "Whose screen debut as Lawrence of Arabia made him an international star?" All three ask the same basic question, but the second two impart something interesting without giving away the answer.

Whatever the subject, you should avoid categories in which *you* happen to be an expert. Unless you're playing someone who is also a buff, you are likely to be blind to what is excessively obscure. For instance, if you know science fiction films inside and out, you might be tempted to throw in stumpers such as, "To which constellation were the *Planet of the Apes* astronauts headed?" (Orion) or "How many minutes pass in *2001: A Space Odyssey* before the first word is spoken?" (twenty-four). Most of your opponents won't want to play with you *or* your opaque questions, and friends who have little interest in the field will be reluctant to swap questions with you. Unless you can do what the philatelist did with the postage stamps—that is, stick to general, relatively mainstream information—it's a good idea to stay away from questions about your own hobbies, profession, etc.

When you have exhausted your supplies of misleading, amusing, trifling, and clue-laden questions, there will still be many questions left to obtain. And since you'll have expended so much ingenuity on the others, it's all right to include a few straightforward queries. Remember, the key to writing questions is diversity of style *and* content. You have already seen to the style; now go through the questions in each category and make certain they're as diversified as possible. If you have created a category called Current Rock Music and find it overladen with The Police or Eurythmics, go and seek out a few questions about Van Halen or ZZ Top. Not only will you learn a few things you didn't know before, but you'll impress people who thought you had pond water for brains.

Mindbenders

Coming up with questions that are trickier than the average Trivial Pursuit questions is one of the joys of writing your own. Trivial Pursuit questions are intended for a broad market, and most people would not be interested in complex, multilevel, or out-and-out trick questions. But if you are playing with a particularly sharp opponent, there is no reason why you can't create a category called PhD—for "Particularly hard to Diagnose." Such a category would be designed specifically (and sadistically) to pose questions such as these:

1. Which doctor is like the number 1,500?
2. Which zodiacal sign is like a person with faulty grammar boasting of jewelry he or she has eaten?
3. Which jungle dweller, turned inside out, is like a '50s Italian actor/singer?
4. What toiletries manufacturer has something in common with Presidents Andy and LB?
5. Which mythological figure can be described as "a wooden leg like you and I"?

The answers are: (1) an M.D.—which would be obvious only to the Roman numerologists among you; (2) Gemini (gem in I); (3) zebra (braze, aka Brazzi); (4) Johnson & Johnson; (5) Pegasus (peg as us). While puzzlers such as these will confound some players, they can also be a refreshing diversion. Extra time can be allowed to solve them, and they can be mandatory for those wizards who tear like cheetahs through every other kind of question.

On the other hand, you don't want to concoct a question so confusing that your opponent cries foul. You could *probably* get away with a query such as "Is Mt. Everest the largest dormant volcano on earth?" (The answer is no, but not because there's one larger...contrary to the question's *implication*, Mt. Everest isn't a dormant volcano.) On the other hand, you'll probably be flogged if you try something such as "Who was the first European to sale across the Atlantic?"—coercing an opponent into answering "Christopher Columbus" when in fact you meant Freddie Laker. You may feel your opponent should have been astute enough to inquire, "Which kind of 'sale'?" But it will be difficult to argue the point when you find your opponent's fist in your mouth.

Whatever kind of trick question you use, make sure you discuss such use ahead of time. While some players may enjoy the challenge, most are understandably likely to resent it.

More Hints for Writing Questions

Trivial Pursuit is not unlike Silly Putty™. The game makers pick up information from other sources and, as we've seen, often stretch it over several cards. You can do the same thing with information you collect. For example, a magazine item or newscast that inspires you to write the question "Which Democrat won the New York Presidential primary in 1984?" should also provide you with data for a question such as "Which Democrat won the Yuppie vote in New York's 1984 Presidential primary?"

When reaching into an event for more than one question, be careful not to give away the answers to succeeding questions. Trivial Pursuit has the advantage of being able to scatter its recycled material over 1,000 questions per category. You don't.

Having suggested this, don't hit the same subject *too* often or your questions will become boring. A large part of the appeal of Trivial Pursuit is not knowing what to expect and having to shift mental gears with every new question. If you're going to write vaguely similar questions, try to use them in separate games.

By the way, there's always the chance that even if you have stocked your larder, you'll *still* manage to run out of new material during the course of a game. Since you won't want to return to old Trivial Pursuit questions, here are some fast ways to dig up questions:

1. Ad-lib questions by running to the nearest dictionary or thesaurus and improvising questions about the category. For example:
   a. Offer your opponent three spellings of an unusual word associated with the category and ask which is correct.
   b. Demand to know a word's Latin or Middle English origins.
2. Many encyclopedias have study questions about various topics. You can ask these.
3. If the category is about historical events, look up a President's name in an encyclopedia or dictionary and ask, "Who was President during the year 1941?" etc. If you're feeling bitchy, ask who was Vice-President during a certain year.
4. Keep copies of *People*, *TV Guide*, *Newsweek*, and/or your local newspaper near the game. This can actually increase the excitement of play, for your

opponent can give *you* thirty seconds in which to come up with a new question or she or he gets to use the colored space as a roll-again space.

5. If all else fails, prior to play, earmark questions in this book or some other volume of trivia—questions that will fit each of your categories. Keep the book handy and jump to it if necessary.

These may not be pretty ways to play but, in a pinch, they can be gamesavers.

How to Barter and Sell Your Trivia Questions

Writing questions for the public is one of the real joys of authoring trivia. Writing questions for friends and family is rewarding, to be sure, but by going public you can turn your hobby into a prosperous little business, the source of new friendships, or a soapbox from which to become a public ham-cum-pseudointellectual. What's especially satisfying about all of this is that age is no barrier: Anyone who can read and write can make trivia a rewarding part of his or her business and social life.

The procedure for creating questions for public consumption is by and large the same as it was when you were writing them for your own use. Computer files or folder files are fine, as long as you keep feeding them information. Again, you don't have to write the questions at once: better to just clip or write down material that seems appropriate, then charge through the writing in a fit of creative passion. The primary difference is that writing questions is no longer something to do only when the fancy strikes you. You have to have discipline if you're going to make trivia personally and/or financially rewarding.

PENPAL TRIVIA

Contacting other trivia buffs by mail is not as difficult as you might think. If you have a hobby, chances are you read a newspaper or journal about that pastime. A classified ad or letter to the editor in such a publication is certain to rally kindred souls, and you're sure to have fun out-trivializing them in a favorite field. If you haven't any hobbies, perhaps there's a specific city you have always wanted to write to or learn more about. Call your local newspaper or library and ask for the name and address of the newspaper in that area. Drop the newspaper a line, ask for classified rates, and make your pitch. If nothing else, the paper will probably do an article about you under the heading "Loon of the Month."

Who knows? Couples have met and fallen in love in many strange ways. It's not inconceivable that you can meet your true love while questioning one another through the mail about the centigrade boiling point of mercury (356.7 degrees) or the number of tentacles the giant octopus had in the 1953 monster movie *It Came from Beneath the Sea*. (Six. The per-tentacle cost of the model was so high that the producers always kept two appendages "underwater.")

TRIVIA AS A BUSINESS

If you are hardhearted, overly rich with friends, or just plain greedy, you might want to go into trivia as a mail-order *business*. Doing so, keep in mind the many specific markets which are ignored by existing trivia card sets and publications. To cite just one example, trivia books have been published about everything from the Olympics to vampires. Yet there are no trivia books and/or columns of questions about stargazing, even though there *is* a widely read magazine on the subject, *Sky and Telescope*. For 50 cents per word you can run a small classified ad. There you can wax enthusiastic about the questions you have written, suggesting that they be purchased for games, diversions at astronomy conventions, sale in planetariums, or just to test the reader's "Sky-Q." If you charge $2 or $3 for 300 questions and manage to sell twenty-five sets a month, you're doing okay—assuming, of course, it didn't take you a decade to come up with questions like "Which is the correct Messier designation for the Trifid nebula?" (M20, in case you could only remember the first 19) and "Where in Australia is the Siding Spring Mountain Observatory?" (Coonabarabran; to help you get your bearings, it isn't far from Warrumbungle National Park).

If astronomy isn't your forte, you can always cook up and advertise cat questions in a publication like *Cat Fancy*, jogging in *Running*, golf in *Golf Digest*, videogames in such periodicals as *Play Meter* and *Electronic Games*, food in *Gourmet*, rock artists in *Rolling Stone*, science fiction in *Isaac Asimov's Science Fiction Magazine*, and chocolate in *Chocolatier*. Nor should you ignore hobbyists who, if they're reading a magazine about their favorite subject, are probably avid enough to want to tackle a trivia quiz. A brief browse around the newsstand will turn up magazines for collectors of coins, comic books, dolls, and even postal cards (not *post* cards, mind you, but those government-issued cards which are too small to let you write anything meaningful).

To summarize: Take a look around, see what magazine captures your interest, write the questions, and take out your ad. However, make sure you go about it in *that* order. The post office takes a dim view of people who wait to see what kind of orders they get before deciding whether or not to produce the goods. Mail fraud is only recommended for those who want *lots* of free time to collect trivia—when they're not busy thwacking out license plates.

Incidentally, you'll be surprised to find that many specialized magazines will actually pay for and publish your questions as a pleasant divertissement for their readers. Some, like *Moviegoer*, actually have regular trivia columns. Drop a note to the editor (enclosing a self-addressed, stamped envelope for their reply) to see if they're interested.

Keep in mind that if you undertake trivia as a business enterprise, while *you* may know that you're honest, your potential customers do not. Thus, give your undertaking a name, such as Trivia Associates or Inconsequentials Ltd. People are more willing to send money to a "company" they've never heard of than to an individual. Make sure, too, that you price your goods low at first. Readers are more likely to send $3 than $20 to a person with whom they've never dealt. After a few months, when you have earned a reputation and readers have become familiar with your ad, you can increase both your charge and the number of questions you produce.

In terms of the appearance of your product, a photocopy of ten or fifteen typed pages may not be classy, but it's the least expensive way to duplicate your material. If the contents are good, the form isn't terribly important. Besides, putting the pages in a folder not only increases the cost of the package but will also send the postage rates through the roof. However, if you're serious about your enterprise and want to produce a quality product at a reasonable cost, shop around for a printing house. Whether you want them to run off your typed page or reset it in type, you can get thousands of copies of your questions for a price between $50 and a few hundred.

If you really get successful and/or ambitious, your next step should be to go after audiences in magazines like *TV Guide* and *Discover*. Your expenses will increase from approximately $15 for a hefty classified ad to $1,500 for a microscopic spot barely distinguishable from a comma. But the size of your audience will increase enormously. If you're game, it may be worth $2,000 or more to mega-jump from a piddling tens of thousands to tens of *millions* of potential customers. Think of it: If 5,000 *Playboy* readers send for your Erotic Trivia Quiz at $5 a throw, you have more than paid for the advertisement.

Keep in mind that by "going big" you'll have one other additional start-up cost. Since most national magazines don't run classifieds, it will be necessary for a local ad/ art agency, typesetter, or even college design student to create an eighth- or quarter-page ad for you. This shouldn't cost more than a $100, and, of course, you can use the same ad over and over.

Don't overlook your own town when selling or bartering trivia. If you live in a big town, something the size of Boston or St. Louis, you probably have a newsstand magazine devoted to that city. Most of these publish classified ads at a reasonable rate, and though you may be sandwiched between ads for gorillagrams and swingers, at least you know your ad will be read. Before you advertise in such publications, it would be a good idea to come up with questions devoted solely to that geographical area. People like to feel that the place they live in is special and may buy your questions strictly out of civic pride. What's more, your advertisement is certain to attract the attention of political, educational, and civic groups who may be interested in using your questions in public forums. Once again, the publication itself may be interested in running the questions you create, so be sure to query them on this.

For those of you who live in smaller towns such as Cowpens, South Carolina, or Itta Bena, Mississippi the local newspaper will serve the same purpose—albeit on a lesser scale. Consider, too, writing questions about the largest industries in your area: Caterpillar tractors in Peoria; Kodak film in Rochester; Pleasantville cashew patties in Pleasantville, New York. Not only is there a built-in audience, but a corporation may buy your questions for its own publicity purposes.

An ideal place to sell trivia questions is at a college, preferably one with a campus where students are land-locked and aching for something to do. If there isn't a school in your town, make an effort to contact the college nearest you. Not only is an ad in a university newspaper inexpensive, but if business starts to boom you can always recruit researchers from among the students.

Finally, don't forget that a cheap but surprisingly effective way of contacting local trivia buffs is to tack an index card (it's tougher than paper) to the bulletin board of a college, house of worship, or grocery store. Broadsides like these may not be fancy, but were good enough to get the American Revolution started. They'll do the job for you too.

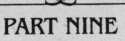

PART NINE

ALL-NEW TRIVIA QUESTIONS TO HELP YOU GET STARTED WRITING YOUR OWN

❧

To say that our appetite for trivia is insatiable is an understatement. For that reason, we offer up the following selection of questions with the hope that they will offer you inspiration in creating your own questions to use while playing Trivial Pursuit.

Instead of using Questions of the same sorts as in Trivial Pursuit, we show many different styles of questions, including multiple-choice questions. Levels are varied, as your own questions should be. Additionally, new categories have been selected.

When writing your own questions, compare them to the ones in this book as well as to the ones in your Trivial Pursuit game. Your best mixture of trivia questions will consist of the seven different types of questions we discussed earlier in this book. Examples of all seven types are shown here.

The categories selected here range from Rock and Roll to Science. Have fun reading through the questions and answers, but while doing so, make notes as to the various ways the questions are asked.

Here are the categories:

Motion Pictures

The emphasis is on who played what, what happened on the screen, and movie titles. Private lives of the stars, among others, are the meat of the Personalities category.

Sports

The well-known sports are here, of course, along with a few even the other trivia games avoided.

Rock and Roll

This grouping deals exclusively with the era of the 1950s through the 1980s, emphasizing "top-forty" hits and the musicians that made them.

TV

Like the Motion Pictures category, everything about what you've seen on the tube, from stars to their roles to their series to words in their theme songs.

Science & Technology

If you have a smattering of knowledge about animals in the wild, outer space, geology, medicine, the human body, inventions, and mathematics, this will be a breeze. If not, an ill wind at the worst.

Personalities

A catch-all category about what people did in fields ranging from feminism to surgery to movies to modeling to art to fashion to politics.

Whatever the category, these questions have been written in all the styles discussed throughout our text, from true/false to multiple-choice to the grossly misleading (in other words, *read them carefully*!). Naturally, we've scrambled up the styles just to keep you from growing complacent. While you're tussling with the answers, study the questions, their diversity, and the way they're worded: They're sure to get the creative juices flowing so that you can write your own!

Motion Pictures: All-New Questions

1. The death of what actor dropped the film role of Dracula into the lap of Bela Lugosi?
2. What sport did Charlton Heston play in *Number One*?
3. What hero of radio and TV fame did Klinton Spilsbury play in 1981?
4. Who said, after winning his Best Actor Oscar in 1968, "Before tonight, I wasn't even considered important enough to be invited"?
5. Name the project which Kirk Douglas starred in on Broadway in 1963 and his son Michael produced as a film in 1975.
6. Name the cartoon feature in which Judy Garland provided the voice of a cat.
7. What actor died halfway through the filming of *Solomon and Sheba*, all of his scenes being reshot with Yul Brynner?
8. How many commandments was Moses given in Mel Brooks' *A History of the World, Part One*?
9. What kind of animal gave Diane Keaton and Woody Allen grief at their *Annie Hall* beach house?
10. Which of the following was *not* a sequel to *The Pink Panther*?
    a. *The Pink Panther's Revenge*
    b. *The Pink Panther Strikes Again*

   c. *Return of the Pink Panther*

11. Who directed John Wayne in *The Alamo*?

12. How many sequels have there been to *Airport*?

13. In which 1962 film did Terry-Thomas and Buddy Hackett play reluctant dragon-killers?

14. What actor scored the last touchdown in *The Longest Yard*?

15. For what supervisory government post was Clark Gable running in *San Francisco*?

16. What movie gimmick was shared by the films *Midway* and *Roller Coaster*?

17. What world-famous journalist narrated the first Cinerama film, *This Is Cinerama*?

18. For which of these late actors was a death scene *not* his final screen appearance?
   a. Edward G. Robinson
   b. Robert Taylor
   c. Ralph Richardson

19. What two U.S. Presidents were portrayed in *Yankee Doodle Dandy*?

20. What did Robert Wagner invent in *Stars and Stripes Forever*?

21. What king did Peter O'Toole play twice, first in *Becket* and then in *The Lion in Winter*?

22. What was Katharine Hepburn's position in *Desk Set*?

23. What film character dies while chasing a bus bearing his true love?

24. What portion of his anatomy did Paul Scofield lose in *A Man for All Seasons*?

25. What was the last film Cary Grant made before his retirement?

26. Which of these actors did *not* appear in *The Muppet Movie*?
   a. Dean Jones
   b. Mel Brooks
   c. Richard Pryor

27. What film is playing when the circus parades through town in Cecil B. DeMille's *The Greatest Show on Earth*?

28. With which hand does King Kong grip the Empire State Building in his final moments?

29. What magazine presented the madcap *Up the Academy*?

30. Which musical selection closes Walt Disney's *Fantasia*?
    a. *The Sorcerer's Apprentice*
    b. *Ave Maria*
    c. *The Rite of Spring*

31. What was the occupation of Burt Reynolds and Goldie Hawn in *Best Friends*?

32. Who played the scarecrow in *The Wiz*?

33. Which witch is killed when Dorothy's house lands in Oz?

34. *The Turning Point* was nominated for eleven Oscars. How many did it win?

35. During the making of *Head* in 1968, what grown-up actor remarked, "Actually, I'm a golfer. That's my real occupation. Ask anybody, particularly the critics."

36. In what city was the heist to take place in *Topkapi*?

37. What actor's most famous film is known in his native tongue as *Shichi-Nin no Samurai*?

38. For whom had Kim Novak's role in *Of Human Bondage* originally been written?

39. What was the first name of Detective Tibbs, played three times by Sidney Poitier?

40. What famous director was for a time Anthony Quinn's father-in-law?

41. What Warren Beatty/Goldie Hawn film didn't have a single letter from the alphabet in its title?

42. To what animal does Ernest Borgnine compare himself in *Marty*?

43. What was emblazoned on the front of Marlon Brando's leather jacket in *The Wild One*?

44. What malady took actor Jeff Chandler's life?

45. What was the name of the first newspaper published by *Citizen Kane*?

46. What is the American name of *Per un Pugno di Dollari*, the Italian flick which made Clint Eastwood a superstar?

47. What shatters when the mermaid squeals her high-pitched *real* name in *Splash*?

48. What does Errol Flynn drop on Prince John's table during the banquet scene in *The Adventures of Robin Hood*?

49. What Danny Kaye film contains a classic tongue twister involving the vessel with the pestle, the chalice from the palace, and the flagon with the dragon?

50. What is the General in Buster Keaton's *The General*?

51. Which actor holds the dubious record of having being nominated for seven Oscars without a single win?

52. What is the longest film title in history?

53. What rough-and-tumble actor was born Charles Buchinsky?

54. What is the historical significance of *Cripple Creek Bar Room*, made in 1898?

55. Who was the first actor to play the Tin Woodsman in an Oz film?

56. What was Humphrey Bogart's middle name?

57. Name the two actresses who have *both* played Queen Elizabeth twice.

58. What Japanese movie featured a giant moth on the rampage?

59. What singer dubbed Lauren Bacall's singing voice in *To Have and Have Not*?

60. What two actresses originated roles in Broadway musicals, only to have Barbra Streisand play them in the movies?

61. What variation of the Trojan Horse is constructed by the intrepid knights in *Monty Python and the Holy Grail*?

62. How many film adaptations have there been of Shakespeare's plays?
    a. 79
    b. 199
    c. 303

63. What actress made her screen debut as a child in *The Happy Land* in 1943?

64. What does the B stand for in Cecil B. DeMille?

65. What was Alfred Hitchcock's last film?

66. What was the only movie Sonny and Cher made together?

67. Who, spurred by general disgust, said during production of the 1970 film which won him a Best Actor Oscar, "I'm not doing too well, and I'm ashamed to be a part of it."

68. Which of these is not a real motion picture?
    a. *Wrestling Women vs. the Aztec Mummy*
    b. *I Dood It!*
    c. *The Johnson County Tomato and Rice Wars*

69. Name the science fiction film directed by *Dallas'* Larry Hagman.

70. What fabled author's screen biography was entitled *A Night in Paradise*?

71. What classic Elizabeth Taylor film was based on F. Scott Fitzgerald's *Babylon Revisited*?

72. How much money did Columbia Pictures pay for the screen rights to the Broadway smash *Annie*?
    a. $2.5 million
    b. $6 million
    c. $9.5 million

73. What singer was originally approached to play the

Kris Kristofferson role in Barbra Streisand's *A Star is Born*?

74. What freckled star's nickname is Dodo?

75. Name the two sequels to *The Bad News Bears*.

76. Whose autobiography is entitled *Wide Eyed in Babylon*?

77. Which film does Paul Newman consider his worst?

78. What future superstar actress appeared as a scantily dressed extra in 1953's *Quo Vadis*?

79. What scientific project was fictionalized in *The Beginning or the End*?

80. What actor founded a production company called the Atticus Corporation?

81. What 1981 movie parody was advertised as "Zany, Zexy, Zensational"?

82. What legendary director played Noah in the 1966 film *The Bible*?

83. In what spaced-out city was Jack Nicholson born?

84. What lethal creatures were known as Maribunta in *The Naked Jungle*?

85. In what film does Lee Marvin play twin brothers?

86. In which film did Burt Lancaster appear briefly in drag?

87. Who did Gene Hackman dress up as in *The French Connection*?

88. What rock star plays the villainous Feyd in the science fiction epic *Dune*?

89. Which of these "twenty million" films doesn't exist?
    a. *Twenty Million Balloons*
    b. *Twenty Million Miles to Earth*
    c. *Twenty Million Sweethearts*

90. It isn't his fault, but what does the Man of Steel repair in *Superman*?

91. What did the special-effects crew use to simulate a locust swarm in *The Good Earth*?

92. In his waning years, what actor said he hoped that

others would one day assess himself thusly: "He was ugly, was strong, and had dignity."

93. What was the X-rated spoof of *2001: A Space Odyssey*?

94. Which Beatle was to be sacrificed in the movie *Help!*?

95. Who played Jackie Robinson in *The Jackie Robinson Story*?

96. How much money did Arthur (in the movie of the same name) stand to inherit?

97. How many times did Laurence Olivier host the Oscars?

98. Which one of these feminine twists on an old theme is the fake?
   a. *Dr. Jekyll and Sister Hyde*
   b. *Lady Scarface*
   c. *Tarzanette*

99. What position did Robert DeNiro play in the baseball movie *Bang the Drum Slowly*?

100. Whose first film was *This Is the Night* in 1932?

MOTION PICTURES: ANSWERS

1. Lon Chaney, Sr.
2. Football
3. The Lone Ranger
4. Cliff Robertson
5. *One Flew Over the Cuckoo's Nest*
6. *Gay Purr-ee*
7. Tyrone Power
8. Fifteen; he dropped five.
9. The Lobster
10. a (The correct title was *Revenge of the Pink Panther*.)

11. John Wayne directed John Wayne in *The Alamo*.
12. Three: *Airport 1974*, *Airport 1977*, and *Airport 1979*
13. *The Wonderful World of the Brothers Grimm*
14. Burt Reynolds
15. City Supervisor
16. Sensurround
17. Lowell Thomas
18. b (Robinson died in *Soylent Green*, Richardson in *Greystoke*.)
19. Theodore Roosevelt and Franklin Delano Roosevelt
20. The sousaphone
21. Henry II
22. She was in charge of the reference library at a television network.
23. Dr. Zhivago
24. His head
25. *Walk, Don't Run*
26. a, Dean Jones
27. Samson and Delilah
28. His right
29. *Mad*
30. b, *Ave Maria*
31. They were screenwriters
32. Michael Jackson
33. The witch of the east
34. None
35. Victor Mature
36. Istanbul
37. Toshiro Mifune
38. Marilyn Monroe
39. Virgil
40. Cecil B. DeMille
41. $
42. A dog
43. "Johnny"

44. Blood poisoning
45. The New York *Daily Inquirer*
46. *A Fistful of Dollars*
47. A row of TV sets
48. A dead buck
49. *The Court Jester*
50. A train
51. Richard Burton
52. *The Persecution and Assassination of Jean-Paul Marat as Performed by the Inmates of the Asylum of Charenton Under the Direction of the Marquis de Sade*
53. Charles Bronson
54. It was the first western motion picture.
55. Oliver Hardy, later of Laurel and Hardy fame, in the silent version of *The Wizard of Oz*
56. DeForest
57. Bette Davis (in *The Private Lives of Elizabeth and Essex* and *The Virgin Queen*) and Flora Robson (in *Fire over England* and *The Sea Hawk*)
58. *Mothra*
59. Andy Williams
60. Carol Channing (*Hello Dolly*) and Barbara Harris (*On a Clear Day You Can See Forever*)
61. The Trojan Rabbit
62. b, 199
63. Natalie Wood
64. Blount
65. *Family Plot*
66. *Good Times*
67. George C. Scott on *Patton*
68. c, *The Johnson County Tomato and Rice Wars*
69. *Beware! The Blob* (aka *Son of Blob*)
70. Aesop
71. *The Last Time I Saw Paris*
72. c, $9.5 million
73. Elvis Presley

74. Doris Day
75. *The Bad News Bears in Breaking Training* and *The Bad News Bears Go to Japan*
76. Ray Milland
77. *The Silver Chalice*
78. Sophia Loren
79. The Manhattan Project: the development of the atom bomb
80. Gregory Peck—named after his character in *To Kill a Mockingbird*
81. *Zorro, the Gay Blade*
82. John Huston
83. Neptune, New Jersey
84. Flesh-eating ants
85. *Cat Ballou*
86. *The Crimson Pirate*
87. Santa Claus
88. Sting
89. a, *Twenty Million Balloons*
90. The San Andreas Fault
91. Coffee grounds stirred in water
92. John Wayne
93. *2069: A Sex Odyssey*
94. Ringo
95. Jackie Robinson
96. $750 million
97. Once, in 1958
98. c, Tarzanette
99. Catcher
100. Cary Grant

Sports: All-New Questions

1. How many more regular-season baseball games did Roger Maris have to slam sixty-one home runs than Babe Ruth had to swat his record sixty?
2. What company provided football's Green Bay Packers with their first uniforms?
3. Name the three brothers who played with the San Francisco Giants in 1963.
4. In what stadium did Billy Jean King defeat Bobby Riggs?
5. What was the sport of brothers Max and Buddy Baer?
6. What did Mark Spitz vow he would become after winning seven gold medals in 1972?
7. How many baseball commissioners have there been?
   a. 13
   b. 9
   c. 6
8. What is the distinction held by Forrest Care "Phog" Allen?
9. In judo, what color is the highest-degree black belt?
10. What event awards the Borg-Warner trophy?
11. What is the home of college football's Pioneer Bowl?
12. In what league do the Argonauts and Alouettes play?
13. In what year was the first Rose Bowl game played?
    a. 1899
    b. 1902
    c. 1913

14. What is a *Yokozuna* in sumo wrestling?
15. What unusual sport required Plennie Wingo to wear special glasses to set his record of 8,000 miles?
16. What gymnastic equipment was perfected and introduced by George Nissen in 1936?
17. How old was tennis prodigy Tracy Austin when she first played at Wimbledon?
18. How many times did Bobby Jones win the U.S. Open?
    a. Twice
    b. Four times
    c. Eight times
19. True or false: The 1980 America's Cup was won by *Courageous*.
20. In what event did Rosie Ruiz misrepresent herself as the winner in 1980?
21. What two soccer federations fought one another in April of 1984 over the right of a player to jump from one to the other?
22. To what group did the New York Yacht Club issue a formal challenge as the first step in winning back the America's Cup, which Australia claimed in 1983?
23. As the only club whose course lies between two active volcanoes, what is policy of Hawaii's Volcano Golf and Country Club if lava sweeps up a player's ball?
24. What Wilt Chamberlain record did Kareem Abdul-Jabbar break in April 1984?
25. Name the first woman to race in the Indianapolis 500.
26. What is the site of the Kentucky Derby?
27. What was the name of the pitcher that Roger Maris hit his sixty-first home run off?
28. True or false: Boxer Leon Spinks, who defeated Muhammad Ali for the heavyweight title in 1978, was a gold medal winner in the Olympics.

29. What was quarterback Roman Gabriel's last team?

30. What National Basketball Association player was the top scorer every season from 1959/1960 through 1965/1966?

31. What is the home state to the NHL Devils?

32. Which team pitched Babe Ruth his sixtieth home run in 1927?

33. What boxer was nicknamed "The Wild Bull of the Pampas"?

34. What was the favorite sport of Sir Thomas Lipton, the tea man?

35. To whom was Brooklyn Dodgers manager Leo Durocher alluding when he uttered his immortal "Nice guys finish last"?

36. In what city did Jackie Robinson play one season of minor-league baseball before "breaking the color barrier" and joining the Brooklyn Dodgers?

37. What was unique about basketballer Rick Barry's freethrow style?

38. How old was hockey legend Gordie Howe when he finally hung up his skates?
    a. 47
    b. 52
    c. 56

39. What did Detroit Tigers catcher Mickey Cochrane suffer from when a pitch was thrown by Irving Hadley in a 1937 game?

40. What classic boxing match did Arthur Donovan referee in June 1938?

41. What jockey rode Zev, Flying Ebony, and Gallant Fox to Kentucky Derby victories in 1923, 1925, and 1930?

42. What was the only team to sneak in one American League pennant victory during the New York Yankees' 1936–1943 reign?

43. In what Ohio city did the Soap Box Derby originate?

44. What college stadium has a seating capacity of over 100,000, the only one which can make that claim?

45. What school produced the first winner of the Heisman Trophy?

46. What was the first team to win the Stanley Cup?

47. Who was the first player to win golf's Masters tournament?

48. Which one of these was *not* a Triple Crown winner?
    a. Omaha
    b. Hoop Jr.
    c. Count Fleet

49. Who did the American Football Coaches Association pick as College Football Coach of the Year in 1978?
    a. Joe Paterno
    b. Don James
    c. Johnny Majors

50. How many goals did the Boston Bruins' Phil Esposito score in his extraordinary 1970/71 season?
    a. 66
    b. 76
    c. 86

51. What nationality was the first winner of the Men's Singles competition at Wimbledon?

52. What kind of car powered Mario Andretti to the Formula 1 Grand Prix championship in 1978?

53. In which sport can you get disqualified for "creeping"?

54. In what sport are Mark Roth, Earl Anthony, and George Pappas top names?

55. What stroke was a specialty of swimmer John Naber?

56. What sport boasts championship matches in "freestyle" and "Greco-Roman" competition?

57. What organization is the keeper of world saltwater fishing records?

58. In what kind of racing will you find the All Amer-

ican Derby, Rainbow Derby, and Kindergarten Futurity?

59. Which football player wrote *I Am Third*?

60. Which one of these is not a National Hockey League trophy?
    a. Hart Trophy
    b. Conn Smythe Trophy
    c. Sanderson Trophy

61. In what sport are Seiji Ono and Anton Stipancic great names?

62. What National Football League team did the Frankford Yellow Jackets eventually become?

63. What player on baseball's St. Louis Cardinals was nicknamed Lippy?

64. What was seen for the last time in the Joe Louis/Abe Simon 1941 heavyweight boxing showdown?

65. For what parabolic pitch was Truett Sewell famous?

66. How many yards did Jim Brown carry the ball during his football career?
    a. 12,312
    b. 13,312
    c. 14,312

67. Who was Don Budge's teammate when he won the Men's Doubles at Wimbledon in 1937 and 1938?

68. What does the James E. Sullivan Memorial Trophy recognize?

69. What was the first name of baseball legend Satchel Paige?

70. How many yards did O. J. Simpson rush in his record-setting 1973 season?
    a. 1,003
    b. 2,003
    c. 3,003

71. Who interrupted Wilbur Shaw's 1937–1940 domination of the Indianapolis 500 championship by winning in 1938?

72. What former New York Knickerbocker was nicknamed Clyde because of sartorial splendor?

73. What was the mascot for the 1980 Winter Olympics in Moscow?

74. Which one of these is not a type of basketball defense?
    a. Zone
    b. Trap
    c. Key

75. Whom did skater Anett Poetzsch beat for the Olympic gold medal?

76. In 1977, what horse became the only undefeated winner of the Triple Crown?

77. The 1982 football strike lasted how many days?
    a. 47
    b. 57
    c. 67

78. True or false: Boxer Gene Tunney lost only one of his seventy-six professional bouts.

79. How many home runs did Hank Aaron belt in his career?

80. How many world records were shattered by runner Jesse Owens on May 25, 1935?

81. How many rounds did it take for Jim Corbett to defeat John L. Sullivan in their 1892 championship slugfest?

82. What city boasts the earliest-known shooting club?

83. Who holds the record for having played the greatest number of consecutive games in the National Football League?
    a. Jim Marshall
    b. Fran Tarkenton
    c. George Blanda

84. What football team was the subject of the 1969 book *The Long Pass*?

85. How many perfect marks did Nadia Comaneci receive in the 1976 Olympics?

86. Which one of these quarterbacks did not play for the Dallas Cowboys?
    a. Craig Morton
    b. Don Meredith
    c. Jim Hart
87. What team is the subject of the book *Eight Men Out*, about the throwing of the 1919 World Series?
88. What Pulitzer Prize play chronicles the triumphs of boxer Jack Johnson?
89. The New York Jets arose from the collapse of what football team?
90. In what year did surfing finally get its own World Championships?
91. What marred Bogdan Norcic's record-breaking 181-meter ski jump in 1977?
92. Do scullers practice their sport in the air, on the water, or on ice?
93. What is played on the largest field of any sport?
94. What are the five events in the pentathlon?
95. True or false: The fastest speed ever achieved in sand-yachting is 113 miles per hour.
96. In what sport is there a quadruple twist lift?
97. What sport did Olympic legend Jim Thorpe play professionally from 1913 to 1919?
98. Who managed the World Series–winning 1969 New York Mets?
99. What was the number of Chicago Bear Gale Sayers?
100. What was raced in the Roll-It Derby during half-time of a 1965 Jets/Raiders game in New York?

SPORTS: ANSWERS

1. Eight
2. The Acme Packing Company
3. Matty, Jesus, and Felipe Alou
4. The Houston Astrodome
5. Boxing
6. A dentist
7. c, 6
8. He was the first person inducted into the Basketball Hall of Fame.
9. Red
10. The Indianapolis 500
11. Wichita Falls, Texas
12. The Canadian Football League
13. b, 1902
14. A Grand Champion
15. Backward walking
16. The trampoline
17. Fourteen
18. b, four times
19. True
20. The Boston Marathon
21. The U.S. Soccer Federation and the Danish Football Federation
22. The Royal Perth Yacht Club
23. It must be played from where it landed before the lava poured in.
24. He scored more career points than any basketball player in history.
25. Janet Guthrie

26. Churchill Downs
27. Tracy Stallard
28. True
29. The Philadelphia Eagles
30. Wilt Chamberlain
31. New Jersey
32. The Washington Senators
33. Luis Firpo
34. Yachting
35. New York Giants manager Mel Ott
36. Montreal
37. He threw underhanded.
38. b, 52
39. A near-fatal concussion
40. The Joe Louis/Max Schmeling bout
41. Earle Sande
42. The Detroit Tigers
43. Dayton
44. Michigan, in Ann Arbor
45. Yale
46. The Ottawa Senators
47. Horton Smith
48. b, Hoop Jr.
49. a, Joe Paterno
50. b, 76
51. French
52. A Lotus
53. Racewalking
54. Bowling
55. The backstroke
56. Wrestling
57. The International Game Fish Association
58. Quarter-horse racing
59. Gale Sayers
60. c, Sanderson Trophy
61. Table tennis
62. The Philadelphia Eagles

63. Leo Durocher
64. A scheduled duration of twenty rounds
65. The Blooper
66. a, 12,312
67. Gene Mako
68. Sportsmanship—outstanding amateur athlete
69. LeRoy
70. b, 2,003
71. Floyd Roberts
72. Walt Frazier
73. Misha the Bear
74. c, Key
75. Linda Fratianne
76. Seattle Slew
77. b, 57
78. True
79. 755
80. Six
81. Twenty-one
82. Geneva, Switzerland
83. a, Jim Marshall
84. The New York Jets
85. Seven
86. c, Jim Hart
87. The Chicago White Sox
88. *The Great White Hope*
89. The Titans
90. 1964
91. Norcic fell on landing.
92. On water
93. Polo
94. Fencing, riding, running, shooting, and swimming
95. False. The record is 57 miles per hour.
96. Skating
97. Baseball
98. Gil Hodges
99. Forty

100. Refrigerators. Eager women won groceries by pushing them across the field at Shea Stadium.

Rock And Roll: All-New Questions

1. How many musicians were there in Paul McCartney and Wings?
2. What is the band's correct name?
   a. ZZ Top
   b. EZ Tops
   c. ZZ Tops
3. Who is the lead singer of the Brooklyn Bridge?
4. True or False: Bob Zimmerman wrote the song *Lay Lady Lay*.
5. Whose first big hit was *I Walk the Line*?
6. *No One Here Gets Out Alive* was a book about what immortal rock group?
7. Who was the shortest member of the Monkees?
8. Which one of these was a Little Richard hit?
   a. *I'm a Man*
   b. *Tutti-Frutti*
   c. *The Purple People Eater*
9. What is the stage name of rock megastar Gordon Summer?
10. Which two Motown supergroups teamed to record *I'm Gonna Make You Love Me* in 1972?
11. Which of these Beatles albums was *not* produced by longtime collaborator George Martin?
    a. *Let it Be*
    b. *Rubber Soul*
    c. *Magical Mystery Tour*

12. The career of what Southern rock band ended in 1977 when three of its members were killed?

13. What group rose from the ashes of the American Breed?

14. What was Elvis Presley's occupation when he cut his first record?

15. What album produced Bonnie Tyler's smash *Total Eclipse of the Heart*?

16. Who recorded the '50s novelty hit *Witch Doctor*?
    a. Sheb Wooley
    b. David Seville
    c. The Playmates

17. What kind of Chameleon did Culture Club sing about on their *Colour by Numbers* album?

18. Where did the Beatles play their last concert?
    a. Shea Stadium
    b. Candlestick Park
    c. Radio City Music Hall

19. Name the town and state in which Elvis Presley was born.

20. Which ex-Beatle played on the Hall and Oates album *Along the Red Edge*?

21. What was the first group to record the '50s standard *Earth Angel*?

22. What was the alliterative title of Dickey Do and the Don'ts' 1958 hit?
    a. *Do, Do, Do, Dear Dora*
    b. *Ne Ne Na Na Na Na Nu Nu*
    c. *C-C-C-Claudia*

23. What group consists of Cy Curnin, Adam Woods, Jamie West-Oram, Danny Brown, and Rupert Greenall?

24. What Sly and the Family Stone record was also a hit for Joan Jett?

25. Who had a hit in 1956 with *I'm In Love Again*?
    a. Fats Domino
    b. Buddy Holly

    c. The Drifters

26. What was the name of the late Marvin Gaye's beloved singing partner?

27. Which group replaces its members once they reach sixteen years of age?

28. How many Luftballons are there?

29. Who originally recorded Tina Turner's March 1984 release *Let's Stay Together*?

30. Which one of these ladies was not featured in a Neil Diamond hit?
    a. Rosie
    b. Caroline
    c. Gloria

31. What, according to Spandau Ballet, is "indestructible"?

32. Who wrote Badfinger's 1970 hit *Come and Get It*?

33. What song appears twice on Bette Midler's album *The Divine Miss M*?

34. What kind of car does Prince sing about?

35. Where did the Partridge Family sing about meeting you in 1971?

36. What did Paul McCartney forget to wear on the cover of the Beatles' album *Abbey Road*?

37. What song was a big 1956 hit for the Heartbeats?

38. What is there "no sign of" in David Bowie's 1983 song *Modern Love*?

39. What was the name of Drifter Bobby Hendricks' first solo hit?
    a. *Beep Beep*
    b. *Sink the Bismarck*
    c. *Itchy Twitchy Feeling*

40. Whom did Gary Puckett and the Union Gap want to give "another chance to show us how to love one another" in 1970?

41. Who had a chart-topper in 1984 called *Yah Mo B There*?

42. According to *Billboard* magazine, what three groups with numbers in their names had top-forty albums in the first half of 1984?

43. What rock superstar broke millions of hearts when he married Valerie Bertinelli of TV's *One Day at a Time*?

44. What twenty-one-year-old punk superstar died of a heroin overdose on Ground Hog's Day, 1979?

45. Which one of these musicians is not a member of Eurythmics?
    a. Annie Lennox
    b. David Stewart
    c. Roy Hay

46. What is Boy George's real name?

47. For which group was "one" the loneliest number?

48. What song was recorded by rock giants John Sebastian, Stephen Stills, and David Crosby?

49. What was the career of Motown founder Berry Gordy before he established the record label?

50. According to Paul Simon, where were Me and Julio?

51. What was the first thing people called the lover/sinner in the 1973 Steve Miller hit *The Joker*?

52. What tune did the Jewels, the Fontane Sisters, and the Charms all record in 1954?

53. What declaration followed "Baby, Now That I've Found You" in the Foundations' 1967 smash of the same name?

54. What was Motown's first number-one hit?

55. Which Monkee wrote Linda Rondstadt's first hit, *Different Drum*?

56. Name the duo that recorded the Oscar-winning chart-topper *Up Where We Belong*.

57. What was Elvis Presley's middle name?

58. What was George Harrison holding on the picture sleeve of his *What Is Life* 45?

59. Which one of these was not a top-ten rock group in 1983?
    a. Men
    b. Men Without Hats
    c. Men at Work

60. What place did Bill Withers sing about on the flip side of his hit 1971 single *Ain't No Sunshine*?

61. Where did Gladys Knight's Midnight Train go?

62. Which one of these songs was not recorded by Al Wilson?
    a. *Show and Tell*
    b. *Touch and Go*
    c. *Kiss and Run*

63. What is "tossed" in the Turtles' 1967 hit *Happy Together*?

64. What was Dinah Washington's huge 1959 hit?

65. What Ray Stevens song opened with children saying a prayer?

66. Who was Peaches' singing partner?

67. What was the name of the group which scored with *They're Coming to Take Me Away, Ha-Ha* in 1966?

68. What is the name of the Pink Floyd album which has been on *Billboard*'s top-200 chart for over ten years?

69. *Infidels* was whose highly praised 1983 album?
    a. The Rolling Stones
    b. Bob Dylan
    c. Stevie Nicks

70. In what country was Joni Mitchell born?

71. How long were the Grassroots willing to wait in their 1973 hit?

72. What group had a 1975 hit entitled *Bohemian Rhapsody*?

73. What lovable TV theme hit the charts with a disco treatment in 1976?

74. Who wrote Kenny Rogers' 1980 hit *Lady*?

75. Name the album that was the source of the Pointer Sisters hit *Slow Hand*.

76. Which one of these Police videos was produced in black and white?
    a. *Every Breath You Take*
    b. *Synchronicity II*
    c. *Wrapped Around Your Finger*

77. True or false: Art Garfunkel wrote the lyrics for *Bridge Over Troubled Water*.

78. Which one of these was Gene Vincent's big 1956 hit?
    a. *I Want You, I Need You, I Love You*
    b. *Splish Splash*
    c. *Be-Bop-A-Lula*

79. What band brought fame and fortune to members Ace Frehley, Peter Criss, Paul Stanley, and Gene Simmons?

80. Who wrote Janis Joplin's superhit *Me and Bobby McGee*?

81. Though he's now a solo performer, what group did Robert Plant ride to prominence?

82. What group wrote a book entitled *Crank Your Spreaders*?

83. Stuart and Clyde are the last names of what popular duo from the '60s?

84. True or false: The debut album of Haircut 100 was entitled *Pelican West*.

85. What was the name of Mike Nesmith's award-winning music/video compilation?

86. Who once said, "I'd rather die than be forty-five and still singing *Satisfaction*"?

87. What Memphis-born songstress is nicknamed the Queen of Soul?

88. What name is singer Reginald Kenneth Dwight better known by?

89. Whose 1977 album *Just the Way You Are* started

this singer on his climb to the rock stratosphere?

90. What was Fleetwood Mac's top-selling album?
91. What is singer Tom Jones' real name?
92. From what country did the Bay City Rollers hail?
93. What did Meat Loaf see by the dashboard light?
94. Which member of Chicago accidentally shot himself to death in 1978?
95. Which Beatle married Linda Eastman in 1969?
96. Who broke out of Big Brother and the Holding Company to become a rock legend?
97. *I Got You Babe* was Sonny and Cher's first hit. What was their second?
98. What was Sam the Sham's backup group?
99. Who is the Grateful Dead's most famous member and gift to guitardom?
100. Who was lead singer for the Temptations from 1964 to 1968?

ROCK AND ROLL: ANSWERS

1. Five
2. a, ZZ Top
3. Johnny Maestro
4. True: Bob Zimmerman changed his name to Bob Dylan.
5. Johnny Cash
6. The Doors
7. Davy Jones
8. b, *Tutti-Frutti*
9. Sting
10. The Temptations and Diana Ross and the Supremes
11. a, *Let It Be*
12. Lynyrd Skynryd
13. Rufus
14. Truck driver
15. *Faster Than the Speed of Night*

16. b, David Seville
17. Karma
18. b, Candlestick Park
19. Tupelo, Mississippi
20. George Harrison
21. The Penguins
22. b, *Ne Ne Na Na Na Na Nu Nu*
23. The Fixx
24. *Everyday People*
25. a, Fats Domino
26. Tammi Terrell
27. Menudo
28. 99
29. Al Green
30. c, Gloria
31. Gold
32. Paul McCartney
33. *Friends*
34. A little red Corvette
35. Halfway
36. His shoes
37. *A Thousand Miles Away*
38. "Life"
39. c, *Itchy Twitchy Feeling*
40. Adam and Eve
41. James Ingram
42. .38 Special, U2, and UB 40
43. Eddie Van Halen
44. Sid Vicious
45. c, Roy Hay
46. George O'Dowd
47. Three Dog Night
48. *She's a Lady*
49. He was a boxer.
50. Down by the schoolyard
51. A space cowboy
52. *Hearts of Stone*

53. "I can't let you go."
54. *Please Mr. Postman*
55. Mike Nesmith
56. Joe Cocker and Jennifer Warren
57. Aron
58. A guitar
59. a, Men
60. Harlem
61. To Georgia
62. c, *Kiss and Run*
63. The dice
64. *What a Difference a Day Makes*
65. *Everything Is Beautiful*
66. Herb
67. Napoleon XIV
68. *Dark Side of the Moon*
69. b, Bob Dylan
70. Canada
71. A million years
72. Queen
73. *I Love Lucy*
74. Lionel Richie Jr.
75. *Black & White*
76. a, *Every Breath You Take*
77. False: Paul Simon wrote the lyrics *and* the music.
78. c, *Be-Bop-A-Lula*
79. Kiss
80. Kris Kristofferson
81. Led Zeppelin
82. The Association
83. Chad and Jeremy
84. True
85. *Elephant Parts*
86. Mick Jagger
87. Aretha Franklin
88. Elton John
89. Billy Joel

90. *Rumours*
91. Tom (Thomas) Jones Woodward
92. Scotland
93. Paradise
94. Terry Kath
95. Paul McCartney
96. Janis Joplin
97. *Baby Don't Go*
98. The Pharaohs
99. Jerry Garcia
100. David Ruffin

TV: All-New Questions

1. What husband-and-wife team starred as *He & She*?
2. What was Mousketeer Lonnie's last name?
3. What was the last name of *Harry-O*?
4. Name the twins Patty Duke played on *The Patty Duke Show*.
5. Who beamed down to star in the short-lived ABC series *Barbary Coast*?
6. Who played the King of Siam in the 1972 flop series *Anna and the King*?
7. Which of the founding fathers was played by Barry Bostwick in a 1984 miniseries?
8. What was the relationship of Penny Marshall to *Laverne & Shirley* producer Garry?
9. What future comic superstar once wrote TV scripts for the Smothers Brothers, Sonny and Cher, and Glen Campbell?
10. What was the name of Lee Marvin's police series?

11. Name the two series in which Sally Field starred.
12. True or false: Andy Devine was one of the stars of *Flipper*.
13. Endora was Samantha's mother on *Bewitched*. Who was her father?
14. Who played Cousin Pearl Bodine on *The Beverly Hillbillies*?
15. Where did Gomer Pyle work in *The Andy Griffith Show*?
16. What was the "extra" possessed by *The Girl with Something Extra*?
17. What was the first name of the character who played the movie star in *Gilligan's Island*?
18. What's the name of the Willis' daughter on *The Jeffersons*?
19. What musical group made monkeys of Ernie Kovacs and company?
20. What was Sergeant Carter's first name in *Gomer Pyle, USMC*?
21. In *The Flintstones*, what was the name of Barney Rubbles' son?
22. What *Lucy Show* star played Mr. Wilson for a single season on *Dennis the Menace*?
23. Who played the *Cowboy in Africa*?
24. What was the name of Commander Adama's son on *Battlestar Galactica*?
    a. Apollo
    b. Starbuck
    c. Boxey
25. What four shows bore the name "Alcoa" in their title?
26. What 1973 series was based on a hit Spencer Tracy/Katharine Hepburn film?
27. Which one of these was not a TV series?
    a. *Action Autographs*
    b. *The Lamb's Gambol*

c. *Willie of Phillie*

28. In what significant way did the TV series *Barefoot in the Park* differ from the stage play?

29. How is Buddy related to Kate in the series *Family*?

30. What was the name of the ship in the TV series *Mr. Roberts*?

31. True or false: Burt Lancaster's son Bill played the young Moses in the 1975 miniseries *Moses—the Law Giver*.

32. What's the name of Oscar's ex-wife on *The Odd Couple*?

33. Did Ryan O'Neal play Norman or Rodney Harrington on *Peyton Place*?

34. Where does Quincy work?

35. What was the name of the Green Hornet's car?

36. What was Ricky Nelson's real first name?

37. On the show *St. Elsewhere*, to what animal is Dr. Ehrlich frequently compared?

38. What adjective did the narrator always utter in conjunction with *Batman*'s Wayne Manor?

39. When, according to the song, did Zorro come "out of the night"?

40. Name the three top-twenty shows in 1968 which had initials in their titles.

41. True or false: *The Monkees* won an Emmy as the Outstanding Comedy Series of 1966–1967.

42. What ex-footballer played a basketball coach on *The Waverly Wonders*?

43. What was Major Adams' first name on *Wagon Train*?

44. What TV dramatic series had a $ in its title?

45. What are the three TV series which have had Dick Van Dyke's name in the title?

46. On whose book was the TV series *The Untouchables* based?

47. Why was *The Ugliest Girl in Town* so ugly?

48. What was Frank Savage's rank in *Twelve O'Clock High*?
49. What *Silkwood* star was featured in the short-lived *Travels of Jamie McPheeters*?
50. What was the special ingredient that Millie purposely left out when she gave Laura her peanut butter dip recipe in *The Dick Van Dyke Show*?
51. Devon Scott played Tony Randall's daughter in *The Tony Randall Show*. Whose daughter is she in real life?
52. What variety series, though laden with brilliant supporting like Michael Keaton, David Letterman, and Swoosie Kurtz, died a quick death in 1978?
53. Which one of these was actually a TV series?
    a. *Tom, Dick, and Harry*
    b. *Tom, Dick, and Mary*
    c. *Tom, Dick, and Larry*
54. Who was the only *To Tell the Truth* panelist to appear from the show's inception in 1956 to its demise in 1967?
55. Who played Dr. Joe Gannon on *Medical Center*?
56. Long before there was Michael Jackson, there was the TV show *Thriller*. Who was the host?
57. What 1964–1965 show costarred David Frost and Buck Henry, among others?
58. What was Ann Marie's last name on *That Girl*?
59. True or false: Natalie Wood made a cameo appearance in the first episode of husband Robert Wagner's *Hart to Hart*.
60. What was the last name of Mr. Ed's master Wilbur?
61. What western featured the character Hop Sing?
62. What short-lived series starred Lorne Greene as a firefighter?
63. What is Dr. Gillespie's first name?
64. Name the actress who died midway through the first season of her series *Eight Is Enough*.

65. On *The Mary Tyler Moore Show*, what tragic affliction almost prevented Mary from accompanying Mr. Grant to an award dinner?
66. What was the number of McHale's PT boat?
67. What was the name of Commissioner McMillan's smart-mouthed maid?
68. What were the full names of Starsky and Hutch?
69. What was the relationship of the two Prestons in the courtroom drama *The Defenders*?
70. What series did Flip Wilson bring to the air in March 1984?
71. Did *Combat* take place before or after D-Day?
72. What malady was shared by the heroes in *A Man Called Shenandoah* and *Coronet Blue*?
73. Who was the star of *Cos*?
74. What was the name of Ed Ames' character on *Daniel Boone*?
75. What city is the setting for *Cheers*?
76. What classic hero served as the basis for Showtime's first continuing adventure series?
77. What is Captain James T. Kirk's middle name in *Star Trek*?
78. What was Gloria Stivic's occupation in the single-season series *Gloria*?
79. What is Matt Houston's favorite food?
80. What is Chachi's last name?
81. What character is Remington Steele's better half?
82. What planet did Matthew Star call home?
83. On *Hill Street Blues*, with whom does Sergeant Belker spend most of his time on the phone?
84. What is the real name of the hospital known as St. Elsewhere?
85. The costars of *Bring 'Em Back Alive* were also the costars of the science fiction film *Tron*. Name them.
86. What was Pat Paulsen's 1970 comedy series called?
87. True or false: Tony Randall and Jack Klugman

played their characters' fathers on an episode of
The Odd Couple.

88. What was the name of the Nat King Cole show?
89. What was the name of Buck Rogers' ambulatory robot companion?
90. What actor plays Bill Bittinger on *The Buffalo Bill Show*?
91. What is the nickname of *The A-Team*'s Templeton Peck?
92. What series featured a genie named Shabu?
93. What is TV spy Lee Stetson better known as?
94. Who created the on-and-gone 1975 Robin Hood sendup *When Things Were Rotten*?
95. Name the long-running sitcom whose lead character was nicknamed Raj.
96. What show did Sweathog Freddie Washington appear on?
97. What is Don Herbert's TV name?
98. Name the *Gunsmoke* veteran who also costarred on NBC's *The Yellow Rose*.
99. What character did Ben Vereen play in the *Roots* miniseries?
100. Who was sealed into a closet when Lucy wallpapered her bedroom in *I Love Lucy*?

TV: ANSWERS

1. Richard Benjamin and Paula Prentiss
2. Burr
3. Orwell
4. Patty and Kathy
5. William Shatner
6. Yul Brynner
7. George Washington

8. They're brother and sister.
9. Steve Martin
10. *M Squad*
11. *Gidget* and *The Flying Nun*
12. True. He played Hap Gorman.
13. Maurice
14. Bea Benadaret
15. Wally's filling station
16. She had ESP.
17. Ginger
18. Jenny
19. The Nairobi Trio
20. Vince
21. Bam Bam
22. Gale Gordon
23. Chuck Connors
24. a, Apollo
25. *Alcoa Hour, Alcoa Presents, Alcoa Theatre, Alcoa Premiere*
26. *Adam's Rib*
27. c, *Willie of Phillie*
28. It aired with an all-black cast.
29. Buddy is Kate's daughter.
30. The U.S.S. *Reluctant*
31. True
32. Blanche
33. Rodney
34. The Los Angeles County Coroner's Office
35. The Black Beauty
36. Eric
37. Pig
38. Stately
39. "When the full moon is bright."
40. *Gomer Pyle, USMC; Mayberry RFD*, and *The FBI*
41. True
42. Joe Namath
43. Seth

44. *Vega$*
45. *The Dick Van Dyke Show, The New Dick Van Dyke Show,* and *Van Dyke and Company*
46. Eliot Ness'
47. Because she was a guy in drag
48. Brigadier general
49. Kurt Russell
50. Mustard
51. George C. Scott
52. Mary Tyler Moore's *Mary*
53. b, *Tom, Dick, and Mary*
54. Kitty Carlisle
55. Chad Everett
56. Boris Karloff
57. *That Was the Week That Was*
58. Marie was her last name, Ann her first.
59. True
60. Post
61. *Bonanza*
62. *Code Red*
63. Leonard
64. Diana Hyland
65. She had a hair bump.
66. 73
67. Mildred
68. Dave Starsky and Ken Hutchinson
69. They were father and son.
70. *People Are Funny*
71. After
72. They both had amnesia.
73. Bill Cosby
74. Mingo
75. Boston
76. Robin Hood
77. Thaddeus
78. She was a veterinarian's assistant.
79. Texas chili

80. Arcola
81. Laura Holt
82. Quadris
83. His mother
84. St. Eligius
85. Bruce Boxleitner and Cindy Morgan
86. *Pat Paulsen's Half a Comedy Hour*
87. True
88. *The Nat King Cole Show*
89. Twiki
90. Dabney Coleman
91. The Face
92. *Just Our Luck*
93. Scarecrow
94. Mel Brooks
95. *What's Happening*
96. *Welcome Back Kotter*
97. Mr. Wizard
98. Ken Curtis
99. Chicken George
100. Ethyl Mertz

Science & Technology: All-New Questions

1. What accounts for 40 percent of the body weight in the average human being?
2. What distinction is held by the *inferior vena cava*?
3. What was performed for the first time on December 3, 1967, at Groote Schuur Hospital?
4. What animal has the heaviest brain?
5. True or false: Certain breeds of salamander have a gestation period of from two to three years.

6. What is acute nasopharyngitis more commonly known as?

7. What single gathering of insects can claim as many as 250 billion members?

8. Who, after riding Friendship 7 into space, said, "I just kept looking at those dozens of instruments and remembering that every one of them was supplied by the lowest bidder"?

9. What is the largest land animal?

10. How deep is the world's deepest ocean?
   a. 36,000 feet
   b. 46,000 feet
   c. 56,000 feet

11. True or false: Mt. Everest is the world's tallest mountain.

12. What famous scientist defended repeated setbacks in the early days of the U.S. space program by carping, "We're doing no worse than Christopher Columbus, who didn't know where he was going when he left, didn't know where he was when he got there, and didn't know where he'd been when he got back"?

13. The cheetah is the fastest land animal for short-distance running. What is the fastest animal for *sustained* running?

14. How many earthquakes are there in the average year?
   a. 10,000
   b. 50,000
   c. 500,000

15. What skydweller has a maximum life span of three hours?

16. Which continent was Pangaea?
   a. Atlantis
   b. The ancient land mass containing all the other continents
   c. None. It's a bacterium.

17. True or false: The Great White Shark is the largest of all sharks.
18. A parallelepiped is:
    a. a solid figure having six sides, each of which is a parallelogram.
    b. a crustacean the top and bottom of whose shell are parallel.
    c. an instrument used to measure the relative speed of sound and light traveling along the same path.
19. What is the heaviest breed of dog?
20. What does the B stand for in Alan B. Shepard, Jr.?
21. What bone do you break when you break your clavicle?
22. What on earth is an astrobleme?
    a. A hypothesized asteroidal life form
    b. A place where an asteroid has struck our planet
    c. A solar flare
23. How many zeroes follow the 1 in a googol?
24. What first-of-its kind farm was opened on Anastasia Island, Florida, in 1892?
25. What is the claim to fame of Lateiki Island?
26. What innovation did the Packard Motor Co. introduce in November 1939?
27. What was broken on October 14, 1947?
28. What travels through space at 66,620 miles per hour?
29. What is unusual about 4.25-acre Craighead lake?
30. True or false: There are eight bytes in a bit.
31. What is a more convenient term for 1/31,556,925,974th of the solar year?
32. What heavenly spectacle can last no longer than seven minutes, thirty-one seconds?
33. What invention was originally known as the velocipede?
34. What popular bedding item was the Simmons Co. the first to manufacture in October 1946?
35. What architectural innovation did scientific re-

search help support when it was successfully introduced in 1796?

36. What is the science of ergonomics?
    a. The drawing of mathematical conclusions
    b. The allotting of money solely for scientific research
    c. The creating of products so that they are most comfortable for use by human beings

37. True or false: Edwin Hubble determined that throughout the universe there is an average of .0000034 gram of matter per cubic centimeter of space.

38. Worried about security, what scientific agency came to be nicknamed by the press as "Never a Straight Answer"?

39. At what point does a user "boot" a computer?
    a. When it breaks down
    b. To start it up
    c. When one is finished using it

40. True or False: The 1815 eruption of the Indonesian volcano Tambora was so violent that the top 4,100 feet of the 13,450-foot mountain were blown away.

41. What does a batrachophobe fear?

42. In the equation $E = mc^2$, what does the c stand for?

43. What does FAX stand for in computer lingo?
    a. Facsimile
    b. File access
    c. Facts

44. What is the first element named on the Periodic Table?

45. What event cracked someone up for the first time in history on May 30, 1896?

46. Which is denser in terms of grams per cubic centimeter, iron or silver?

47. Alphabetically speaking, is zinc the last element?

48. What substance does the enzyme sucrase act upon?

49. Where in the human body is the ciliary muscle found?
50. What is the common name of sodium hydrogen carbonate?
51. What is the only element that ends in a *y*?
52. To date, how many species of birds have been catalogued?
    a. 6,733
    b. 7,733
    c. 8,733
53. When gravity flung Apollo 8 around the moon and back toward earth, who did pilot William Anders say was driving?
54. What is I/O to a computer programmer?
    a. Information/Organization
    b. Input/Output
    c. Instruction/Operation
55. Ironically, in what year was the first electric stock quotation board installed?
56. With what invention did Melville Bissell clean up in 1876?
57. True or false: Dogs "perspire" through their mouths
58. Quantum physics does not go against one of these pillars of old science:
    a. Dualism
    b. Determinism
    c. Causality
59. True or false: Twentieth-century humans have eaten the meat of extinct mastodons.
60. What is presently the ninth planet from the sun?
61. The phylum Protozoa consists of:
    a. sponges.
    b. starfishes and sea urchins.
    c. single-celled animals.
62. True or false: The element krypton was so named in honor of Superman's home planet.
63. Are marsupials born inside their mother's pouch?

64. What geological period predates the archeozoic?
65. A year on Mercury is:
    a. 78 days
    b. 88 days
    c. 99 days
66. "Bang" is computer jargon for what punctuation mark?
67. What famous scientist was the son of Vincenzio Galilei?
68. What marker tells you where you are on a computer screen?
69. What famous underground formation was discovered by a farmer while plowing his field?
70. What kind of storm is an haboob?
71. True or false: Pencil lead is made from a soft kind of lead named maleum.
72. In terms of volume, how much of 100-proof alcohol is actually alcohol?
    a. 25 percent
    b. 50 percent
    c. 100 percent
73. Is it fission or fusion in which the nucleus of an atom is split?
74. "Conifer" describes what kind of evergreen tree?
75. What is measured by the Beaufort Scale?
76. What is the fastest a gila monster can travel, given a downhill surface and favoring wind?
    a. 2 mph
    b. 5 mph
    c. 7 mph
77. What was once described as the only component of a spacecraft that can be "mass-produced with unskilled labor"?
78. Which color of the spectrum is closer to violet?
    a. Red
    b. Orange
    c. Yellow

79. How many sides does a tetragon have?
80. What part of the Viking 1 spacecraft was visible in the first photograph taken on the surface of Mars?
81. True or false: The eye of the whale is larger than that of any other living creature.
82. Who designed the first successfully implanted artificial heart?
83. Vestigial is a term which describes:
    a. a virgin.
    b. a degenerated part of an organism.
    c. a tail.
84. Aside from being an amateur botanist, what was Gregor Mendel's other profession?
85. Was Copernicus the scientist's first or last name?
86. What is the familiar name of the calcareous skeleton secreted by certain anthozoans?
87. In an unbent posture, which one of these bones is closest to the shoulder?
    a. Patella
    b. Radius
    c. Tarsals
88. With what U.S. university was Albert Einstein long associated?
89. What four-letter word describes impure silicon dioxide?
90. Which planet has twenty-one known moons, the most of any world in the solar system?
91. Anticipation for what book of science was so high that the first printing sold out in one day?
92. A young kangaroo is a joey; what is a young eel called?
93. Is a crocodile a reptile or an amphibian?
94. Seconal is considered:
    a. a depressant.
    b. a tranquilizer.
    c. a hallucinogen.

95. True or false: The black widow is the insect kingdom's deadliest animal.

96. The prehistoric archaeopteryx was the first true what?

97. What are the three kingdoms of nature?

98. Which one of these is the only planet with a moon?
    a. Mercury
    b. Pluto
    c. Venus

99. True or false: You would weigh less on the top of a mountain than at sea level.

100. Which doctor wrote *Everything You Always Wanted to Know About Sex But Were Afraid to Ask?*
    a. Dr. Peter Hauser
    b. Dr. Peter Kaufman
    c. Dr. David Reuben
    d. Dr. Robert Siegel
    e. Dr. Alex Comfort

SCIENCE & TECHNOLOGY: ANSWERS

1. Muscles
2. It's the largest vein in the human body.
3. A heart transplant
4. The sperm whale
5. True
6. The common cold
7. A locust swarm
8. John Glenn
9. The African Bush Elephant
10. a, 36,000 feet
11. False; it's the world's *highest* mountain. From base to tip, Hawaii's Mauna Kea is taller by 4,448 feet.
12. Wernher von Braun
13. The antelope (pronghorn)

14. c, 500,000
15. A rainbow
16. b, the ancient land mass containing all the other continents.
17. False. The Whale Shark is bigger.
18. a, a solid figure having six sides, each of which is a parallelogram.
20. Bartlett
21. Your collar bone
22. b, a place where an asteroid has struck our planet
23. One hundred
24. An alligator farm
25. It is the world's newest, born in 1979.
26. Automobile air conditioning
27. The sound barrier
28. The earth
29. It's entirely underground.
30. False. The reverse is true.
31. A second
32. A solar eclipse
33. The bicycle
34. The electric blanket
35. The suspension bridge
36. c, the creating of products so that they are most comfortable for use by human beings
37. False. His figure was .00000000000000000000000000000001.
38. NASA
39. b, to start it up
40. True
41. Frogs
42. The speed of light
43. a, facsimile
44. Hydrogen
45. An automobile accident
46. Silver
47. No. Zirconium is.

48. Sucrose
49. The eye
50. Baking soda
51. Mercury
52. c, 8,733
53. Isaac Newton
54. b, Input/Output
55. 1929, the year the market crashed
56. The carpet sweeper—the Bissell Broom
57. True
58. a, dualism
59. True. Frozen specimens were unearthed and consumed in Russia.
60. Neptune. Because of the unusual orbits of Neptune and Pluto, it will be so for some years to come.
61. c, single-celled animals
62. False. The opposite is true.
63. No. They have to crawl to her pouch after birth.
64. None
65. b, 88 days
66. An exclamation point
67. Galileo
68. The cursor
69. Howe Caverns
70. A duststorm
71. False. It's graphite, a form of carbon.
72. b, 50 percent
73. Fission
74. Cone-bearing
75. Wind strength
76. a, 2 mph
77. The human occupant
78. c, yellow
79. Four
80. Its footpad
81. False. The honor falls to the eye of the squid.
82. Dr. Robert Jarvik

83. b, a degenerated part of an organism
84. Monk
85. Last. His first name was Nicolaus.
86. Coral
87. b, radius
88. Princeton
89. Sand
90. Saturn
91. Charles Darwin's *The Origin of Species*
92. An elver
93. A reptile
94. a, a depressant
95. False. Spiders aren't insects.
96. Bird
97. Animal, vegetable, and mineral
98. b, Pluto
99. True
100. c, Dr. David Reuben

Personalities: All-New Questions

1. Who rode the ill-fated Skycycle X-2?
2. Which one of these film stars was on an Irish boxing team in the Olympics?
   a. Richard Harris
   b. Errol Flynn
   c. Michael Redgrave
3. What religion is Idi Amin's?
4. What is the first name of cookieman "Famous" Amos?
5. What sport does baseballer Johnny Bench play to relax?

6. How much money was Peter Benchley paid for *Jaws*?

7. Whose professional musical career began when he filled in for an under-the-weather Bruno Walter?

8. What smooth-mover was born Frederick Austerlitz?

9. What is former diplomat Shirley Black's maiden name?

10. What state did Anita Bryant represent in the Miss America contest?

11. Name the author of the newspaper column *On the Right*.

12. Who is Caroline Louise Marguerite?

13. Who presented the Best Picture Oscar at the April 1984 Academy Awards ceremony?

14. What man's five-year boycott against grapes, among other produce, lead to a farmworkers union?

15. What religion is Romanian Nadia Comaneci?

16. What anchor of journalism began his career as a reporter for the Houston *Post*?

17. What Communist activist did a California jury acquit of conspiracy, kidnapping, and murder in 1972?

18. Who was Franklin Delano Roosevelt's psychic adviser?

19. What caused actor Peter Falk to lose his eye?

20. Which first lady was once married to a furniture salesman?

21. Who was the founder of the National Organization of Women?

22. Who is married to the Governor of Kentucky?

23. Billy Frank is the nickname of what religious leader?

24. What designer made a name for himself by designing Jackie Kennedy's famous off-white "pillbox" hat?

25. What kind of plane did Hugh Hefner turn into his private *Big Bunny*?

26. Who was Fabergé's "Babe"?

27. What baseball slugger and confection magnate once quipped, "I'd rather hit than have sex"?

28. Which of these men was the youngest when elected Pope?
    a. John Paul I
    b. John Paul II
    c. John XXIII

29. What Arab leader called Ayatollah Ruhollah Khomeini "a lunatic and a disgrace to Islam"?

30. What senator has made national health care his pet project?

31. What designer's daughter, Marci, was kidnapped in 1978?

32. What newspaper columnist's nickname is Eppie?

33. What musician began his career as the pseudonymous Walter Busterkeys?

34. Who was skiing champion Spider Sabich's last girlfriend?

35. What Northern California poet sold pint after pint of his blood to support himself while he wrote?

36. Who defected in 1961 by throwing himself into the arms of a gendarme and screaming "I won't go back!"?

37. Which astronaut's wife refused to let Lyndon Johnson through her door?

38. Which actress/model/singer named her son Elijah Blue?

39. Who is older, Jackie Onassis or sister Lee?

40. Which Onassis was killed in a plane crash?

41. What does Ronald Reagan superstitiously bowl down the aisle of an airplane before it takes off?

42. To which of these fortunes is actress Dina Merrill not an heir?
    a. E.F. Hutton
    b. Getty Oil
    c. Post cereal

43. The death of what famous designer thrust his assistant, Yves St. Laurent, into the limelight?

44. True or False: Charles Schulz lives on a street called Linus Lane.

45. The death of his wife Joan inspired what Neil Simon play?

46. The first name of what actor/athlete/huckster is Orenthal?

47. Who met a world leader at the Tahiti Club Med and later married him?

48. Why did Thomas Lanier Williams choose Tennessee for his nickname?

49. Who painted *Christina's World*, which has sold more reproductions than any other American painting?

50. Which automobile executive was responsible for having created the Mustang?
    a. John DeLorean
    b. Henry Ford
    c. Lee Iacocca

51. Who introduced the topless bathing suit in the '60s?

52. Who caused a national outcry when he picked up a beagle by the ears and made it squeal?

53. Who were Jane and Joan Boyd?

54. True or false: "They Can't Lick Our Dick" was a Richard Nixon campaign button.

55. Which one of these women was not a Miss America?
    a. Judith Scott
    b. Donna Axum
    c. Judi Ford

56. What car was the most famous creation of customizer George Barris?

57. Whom did General Electric hire in the '60s to create a series of clocks which included such designs as "Daisy Reflection," "Wow Now," and "Opticon"?

58. What black activist wrote the introduction to Jerry Rubin's book *Do It*?

59. What company did Nolan Bushnell sell to Warner Communications for $28 million?

60. Who created and played the TV characters Percy Dovetonsils, Wolfgang Saurbraten, and Pierre Ragout?

61. What writer insisted in several bestsellers that the earth has been visited by benign aliens?

62. What hard-driving millionaire once fumed, "History is bunk"?

63. Back in 1911, Galbraith P. Rodgers was the first man to successfully undertake what journey?

64. What was pharmacist John S. Pemberton's contribution to the grocery shelves?

65. What Princeton graduate wrote *Unsafe at Any Speed: The Designed-In Dangers of the American Automobile*?

66. Who were Albert, Alfred, Charles, John, and Otto?

67. What, in 1859, was Edwin Drake the first to drill?
    a. An oil well
    b. A tooth
    c. A diamond

68. What city has had both Frank Rizzo and Wilson Goode as mayors?

69. Whose interview with Richard Nixon aired on CBS in April 1984?

70. Which doctor won a Pulitzer Prize in 1984?

71. What four-term Idaho senator died on April 7, 1984?

72. What is the name of the Maine youth who visited the Soviet Union at the invitation of Yuri Andropov?

73. To which member of a foreign monarchy is Nancy Reagan related?

74. Who served on the U.S. Supreme Court longer than any other justice in history?

75. What did Alexander Fleming do to make medical history?

76. What was Giovanni Battista Montini better known as?

77. Who told Ernest Hemingway, "You are all a lost generation"?

78. Whose day does Louisiana celebrate on August 30?

79. What was unusual about the way Leonardo da Vinci wrote?

80. What longtime labor leader stepped down in September 1979?

81. Who is Carrie Fisher's mother?

82. Which First Lady whispered in her husband's ear, "Oh Bunny, you're President now"?

83. Who was the first Irish political prisoner to fast to death in Belfast's Maze Prison?

84. Which record company and computer company are named after the same food?

85. What character did Oreste Baldini play in the movies?

86. Who was John Anderson's running mate in 1980?

87. Which of Lloyd Bridges' sons was named after Melanie's boy in *Gone with the Wind*?

88. What former world leader was born in Brest-Litovsk, Poland?

89. What is Antonio Dominick Benedetto's theme song?

90. Which one of these is not a member of the Beach Boys?
    a. Al Wilson
    b. Al Jardine
    c. Mike Love

91. True or false: Burt Lancaster was born Issur Demsky.

92. From what college did *Roots* author Alex Haley graduate?

93. What entertainer was hounded by the FBI after

telling Lady Bird Johnson just what she thought of the war in Vietnam?

94. What is Cheryl Stoppelmoor's married name?
95. What actor/director's first wife was Jackie Witte?
96. Who was so excited to receive an ovation during a stock production of *Hello Dolly* that she shouted, "Wow, look at the dingbat now!"?
97. What singer was born La Donna Andrea Gaines?
98. Whom did Lyndon Johnson refer to as "Rover Boy, without birth control"?
99. What actress spent the latter part of the 1970s on an estate in Middleburg, Virginia?
100. Who starred as Texas John Slaughter and wrote *The Other*?

PERSONALITIES: ANSWERS

1. Evel Knievel
2. b, Errol Flynn
3. Islam (the Muslim religion)
4. Wally
5. Bowling
6. $1,000
7. Leonard Bernstein
8. Fred Astaire
9. Temple
10. Oklahoma
11. William F. Buckley, Jr.
12. Princess Caroline of Monaco
13. Frank Capra
14. Cesar Chavez
15. Atheist
16. Walter Cronkite
17. Angela Davis
18. Jeane Dixon

19. A malignant tumor
20. Betty Ford
21. Betty Friedan
22. Phyllis George
23. Billy Graham
24. Halston
25. A DC-9
26. Margaux Hemingway
27. Reggie Jackson
28. b, John Paul II
29. Anwar Sadat
30. Edward M. Kennedy
31. Calvin Klein
32. Ann Landers
33. Liberace
34. Claudine Longet
35. Rod McKuen
36. Rudolf Nureyev
37. John Glenn's wife, Annie Glenn
38. Cher
39. Jackie
40. Alexander
41. An orange
42. b, Getty Oil
43. Dior
44. False. He lives at Snoopy Place.
45. *Chapter Two*
46. O.J. Simpson
47. Margaret Trudeau
48. His forebears came from that state.
49. Andrew Wyeth
50. c, Lee Iacocca
51. Rudy Gernreich
52. Lyndon Baines Johnson
53. The first Doublemint twins
54. True
55. a, Judith Scott

56. TV's Batmobile
57. Peter Max
58. Eldridge Cleaver
59. Atari
60. Ernie Kovacs
61. Erich von Daniken
62. Henry Ford
63. He was the first to fly America from coast to coast.
64. Coca-Cola
65. Ralph Nader
66. The Ringling brothers
67. a, an oil well
68. Philadelphia
69. Frank Gannon
70. Dr. Seuss
71. Frank Church
72. Samantha Smith
73. Princess Diana. They are tenth cousins.
74. William O. Douglas
75. He discovered penicillin.
76. Pope Paul VI
77. Gertrude Stein
78. Huey P. Long's
79. He used mirror-writing.
80. George Meany
81. Debbie Reynolds
82. Jacqueline Kennedy
83. Bobby Sands
84. Apple
85. Vito Corleone as a boy
86. Patrick Lucey
87. Beau
88. Menachim Begin
89. *I Left My Heart in San Francisco*. Benedetto is better known as Tony Bennett.
90. a, Al Wilson
91. False. That was Kirk Douglas.

92. None
93. Eartha Kitt
94. Ladd.
95. Paul Newman
96. Jean Stapleton
97. Donna Summer
98. Robert Kennedy
99. Elizabeth Taylor
100. Tom Tryon

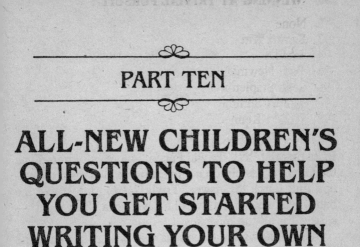

PART TEN

ALL-NEW CHILDREN'S QUESTIONS TO HELP YOU GET STARTED WRITING YOUR OWN

In its first four sets, Trivial Pursuit ignored children. *Time the Game*™ has children's questions which even grown-ups find tough to answer. Trivia Adventure,™ like the baby bear's porridge, would have been "just right"—except for all the mistakes.

What follows are questions that will help you write your own questions for children. Because children advance at different speeds, no attempt has been made to grade the questions in terms of difficulty. When you write your own questions, you might want to gear them for a particular child's level.

While writing your own questions, keep in mind that children have a low tolerance for frustration and will not want to keep answering questions if they keep getting the answers wrong. If you want to write informative, educational questions for your children, make sure they can also get some of the answers right the first time they play.

Best of all, get your children to write their own questions for Trivial Pursuit. They'll learn more . . . and you'll have less work to do.

U.S. Geography: All-New Questions

1. Washington, D.C., is home to what world leader?
2. What is the largest American state?
3. Name two adjoining states that have "New" in them.
4. Which state is home to the Grand Canyon?
5. What state's capital is Hartford?
6. What city is called the Mile High City?
7. In what state is Jimmy Carter's hometown of Plains?
8. Which two states are not part of the continental United States?
9. Where is Mt. McKinley?
10. What state produced the first lollipop?
11. What was the first state to ratify the Constitution?
12. What is the smallest state?
13. Which state is called the Sunshine State?
14. What is the newest state?
15. What state is called the Land of Lincoln
16. Which one of these is not a New England state?
    a. New York
    b. New Hampshire
    c. Massachusetts
17. What is the nickname of Kentucky?
18. In what ocean do the Hawaiian Islands lie?
19. What state forms the northeast corner of the United States?
20. Which state is abbreviated Pa.?
21. Which state is split by Chesapeake Bay?
22. What does D.C. stand for in Washington, D.C.?

23. Fill in the blank: Philadelphia is the City of ———— Love.
24. Name the five Great Lakes.
25. How many *s*'s are there in Mississippi?
26. True or false: Florida was one of the original thirteen colonies.
27. What are Minnesota's twin cities?
28. What is unique about Lake Mead?
29. What's the only state that touches Maine?
30. Which one of these states does not border Washington, D.C.?
    a. Virginia
    b. Maryland
    c. Delaware
31. Is Antarctica the North Pole or the South Pole?
32. Where are the Carlsbad Caverns?
33. Mt. Rushmore is in what state?
34. What state is home to the Great Salt Lake?
35. What is the Garden State?
36. What is the only New England state without a seacoast?
37. Which U.S. river carries the most water?
38. Wyoming, Montana, and Idaho all contain part of what famous park?
39. How often does the geyser Old Faithful erupt?
    a. Once an hour
    b. Once a day
    c. Once a year
40. Where is Pearl Harbor, site of the infamous Japanese surprise attack in 1941?
41. Where is the Lincoln Memorial?
42. True or false: The Statue of Liberty was built in the United States.
43. What are the colors of the U.S. flag?
44. In what city is Central Park located?
45. Which state is longer, California or Florida?

46. Which two states have four straight borders?
47. Which state is nearest to Cuba?
48. What two states have the word "North" in their names?
49. Which state is home to Buffalo, Rochester, and Syracuse?
50. What is the capital of California?
    a. Los Angeles
    b. Sacramento
    c. San Francisco

U.S. GEOGRAPHY: ANSWERS

1. The President of the United States
2. Alaska
3. New York and New Jersey
4. Arizona
5. Connecticut
6. Denver, Colorado
7. Georgia
8. Hawaii and Alaska
9. Alaska
10. Connecticut
11. Delaware
12. Rhode Island
13. Florida
14. Hawaii
15. Illinois
16. a, New York
17. The Bluegrass State
18. The Pacific
19. Maine
20. Pennsylvania

21. Maryland
22. District of Columbia
23. Brotherly
24. Erie, Huron, Ontario, Michigan, and Superior
25. Four
26. False
27. Minneapolis and St. Paul
28. The largest human-made lake in the United States
29. New Hampshire
30. c, Delaware
31. The South Pole
32. In New Mexico
33. South Dakota
34. Utah
35. New Jersey
36. Vermont
37. The Mississippi
38. Yellowstone National Park
39. a, once an hour
40. Hawaii
41. Washington, D.C.
42. False. It was built in France.
43. Red, white and blue
44. New York City
45. California
46. Wyoming and Colorado
47. Florida
48. North Dakota and North Carolina
49. New York
50. b, Sacramento

Science:
All-New Questions

1. How many days are there in the average year?
2. What kind of doctor helps sick animals?
3. Name the four seasons.
4. What was the biggest meat-eating dinosaur?
5. Which month has the fewest days?
6. What is paper made from?
7. What are the five senses?
8. What is the informal name of the electrical term "amperes"?
9. Name the four kinds of taste.
10. What is the name of the threadlike substance we use to clean between our teeth?
11. What is the average temperature of the human body?
12. What is a settlement of ants called?
13. What kind of planes have no engine?
14. What does the abbreviation "mph" mean?
15. Were people alive when the earth was ruled by dinosaurs?
16. Do snakes have tongues?
17. What is the center of the earth called?
18. How many known planets are there in the solar system?
19. How many sets of teeth does the average person get during his or her life?
20. True or false: Crocodiles come from eggs.
21. What is made up of protons, neutrons, and electrons?
22. How many families of rock are there?
23. What does "dinosaur" mean?
24. What does a thermometer measure?

25. What are the four points on a compass?
26. Name the third planet from the sun.
27. What kind of tea is naturally caffeine-free?
28. Who is considered the Father of Evolution?
29. Who is Sally Ride?
30. Who invented the process used to pasteurize milk?
31. What planet is known as the Red Planet?
32. At what Fahrenheit temperature does water freeze?
33. Who invented the light bulb?
34. What percentage of the earth is covered with water?
    a. 20 percent
    b. 40 percent
    c. 70 percent
35. What is H_2O?
36. What is sodium chloride better known as?
37. What is the largest planet in the solar system?
38. What percentage of the human body is water?
    a. 10 percent
    b. 50 percent
    c. 70 percent
39. At what Fahrenheit temperature does water boil?
40. What do Phobos and Deimos revolve around?
41. What kind of animal is a canine?
42. What kind of pull is measured in "g"s?
43. Is the earth closest to the sun during summer or winter?
44. What can't people see if they're nearsighted?
45. What does a praying mantis eat?
46. What's the name of the North Star?
47. Where does pollen come from?
48. What do botanists study?
49. What was Tranquillity Base?
50. Which is longer a foot or a meter?

SCIENCE: ANSWERS

1. 365
2. A veterinarian
3. Winter, spring, summer, fall
4. Tyrannosaurus
5. February
6. Trees
7. Touch, taste, smell, sight, hearing
8. Amps
9. Sweet, sour, salt, bitter
10. Dental floss
11. 98.6 degrees (Fahrenheit)
12. A colony
13. Gliders
14. Miles per hour
15. No
16. Yes
17. The core
18. Nine
19. Two
20. True
21. An atom
22. Three (igneous, metamorphic, sedimentary)
23. "Terrible lizard"
24. Changes in temperature
25. North, south, east, and west
26. Earth
27. Herbal
28. Charles Darwin
29. The first American woman in space

30. Louis Pasteur
31. Mars
32. Thirty-two degrees
33. Thomas Edison
34. c, 70 percent
35. Water
36. Salt
37. Jupiter
38. c, 70 percent
39. 212 degrees
40. Mars
41. A dog
42. Gravity
43. Winter
44. Objects that are far away
45. Insects
46. Polaris
47. Flowers (flowering plants)
48. Plants
49. The landing site of Apollo XI, the first moon mission
50. A meter

The Arts:
All-New Questions

1. What musical instrument has eighty-eight keys?
2. Who wrote *The Cat in the Hat*?
3. On what planet was Luke Skywalker raised?
4. Who were Dorothy, the Scarecrow, the Tin Man, and the Cowardly Lion off to see?
5. Who wrote the play *Romeo and Juliet*?
6. What incredible superhero does Bruce Banner become?

7. Who is He-Man's archenemy?
8. Who are Bo and Luke?
9. Who was Tom Sawyer's girlfriend?
10. What magazine features the comic strip Spy vs. Spy?
11. On *Sesame Street* who is Bert's roommate?
12. What was the last name of Peter Pan's friends Wendy, John, and Michael?
13. Who is the most famous movie vampire?
14. What is the name of Mickey Mouse's dog?
15. What is the name of Gretel's brother?
16. Who was able to spin straw into gold?
17. Whose has an enemy named Oil Can Harry?
    a. Mighty Mouse
    b. Batman
    c. Pac-Man
18. Whom does Vixen work for?
19. Whom did the Oompa Loompas work for?
20. What did Aladdin find in the magic lamp?
21. In what century did Buck Rogers wake up?
22. What is the name of Batman's butler?
23. Who is the lead singer of the Police?
24. What secret agent is known as 007?
25. Who carried Ann Darrow up the side of the Empire State Building?
26. Which of Walt Disney's seven dwarfs couldn't speak?
27. Who was the drummer for the Beatles?
28. Which was the evil one, Dr. Jekyll or Mr. Hyde?
29. Who is Donald Duck's girlfriend?
30. What kind of animal is Dumbo?
31. What is Japan's most famous monster?
32. What famous painter cut off one of his ears?
33. Who is Luke Skywalker's sister?
34. True or false: In the novel *Frankenstein*, Dr. Frankenstein also created a bride for his monster.
35. What is the name of the Lone Ranger's horse?
36. Who painted the *Mona Lisa*?

37. For what instrument did Chopin write most of his music?
38. What is the first name of *Star Trek*'s Captain Kirk?
39. What is the name of the one-legged captain who chases Moby Dick?
40. According to the song in *Snow White and the Seven Dwarfs*, what should you do "while you work"?
41. What character does Mr. T play on *The A-Team*?
42. Who wrote the national anthem of the U.S.A.?
43. What is a nonfiction movie called?
44. Who is the conductor of the Boston Pops?
45. Who sculpted statues of Moses and David?
46. Who wrote *The Raven* and *The Fall of the House of Usher*?
47. What was Beethoven's full name?
48. Where does Tron live?
49. What comic strip features Linus and Lucy?
50. Who painted the picture generally known as *Whistler's Mother*?

THE ARTS: ANSWERS

1. The piano
2. Dr. Seuss
3. Tatooine
4. The Wizard of Oz
5. William Shakespeare
6. The Incredible Hulk
7. Skeletor
8. *The Dukes of Hazzard*
9. Becky Thatcher
10. *Mad*
11. Ernie
12. Darling
13. Dracula
14. Pluto
15. Hansel

16. Rumpelstiltskin
17. a, Mighty Mouse
18. Santa Claus
19. Willy Wonka
20. A genie
21. The twenty-fifth
22. Alfred
23. Sting
24. James Bond
25. King Kong
26. Dopey
27. Ringo Starr
28. Mr. Hyde
29. Daisy
30. An elephant
31. Godzilla
32. Vincent van Gogh
33. Princess Leia Organa
34. True
35. Silver
36. Leonardo da Vinci
37. Piano
38. James
39. Ahab
40. Whistle
41. B.A. Baracus
42. Francis Scott Key
43. A documentary
44. John Williams
45. Michelangelo
46. Edgar Allan Poe
47. Ludwig van Beethoven
48. Inside a computer
49. *Peanuts*
50. Whistler (James Abbott McNeill Whistler)

Toys and Products:
All-New Questions

1. On what day does Hostess sell green Sno-balls?
2. How many colors are there in the biggest Crayola box?
3. Who manufactures ColecoVision?
4. Who is "A real American Hero"?
5. "Where's the beef?" is the slogan of what restaurant?
6. What doll is packaged with a single white glove?
7. What is the strongest piece in checkers?
8. What is table tennis more commonly known as?
9. What kind of animal eats Trix?
10. What is the name of the hero in *Pitfall*?
11. Who is Count Chocula's pink friend?
12. Which comes first in Candyland, ice cream or candy canes?
13. What snack comes with a prize in every box?
14. What baby doll comes with its own birth certificate?
15. What kind of cookie has a message inside?
16. What are the numbers of the two Atari videogame systems?
17. Name the three Rice Crispies elves.
18. What was the first arcade videogame called?
19. What is the strongest piece in chess?
20. Who is Ken's girlfriend?
21. Which ice cream store boasts of having thirty-one flavors?
22. What group of toys do Bakatak and Drrench belong to?
23. Who is Pokey's bendable master?

24. What kind of dessert does Bill Cosby like best?
25. How many railroads are there in Monopoly?
26. What is the name of the Pillsbury Dough-boy?
27. What company makes a computer called the 64?
28. Which one of these is not a candy *bar*?
    a. Milky Way
    b. Snickers
    c. Starburst
29. Who lives in Care-a-lot?
30. What do phosphorescent toys do?
31. How much did the first comic book cost?
32. What does Schwinn make?
    a. Bicycles
    b. Records
    c. Computers
33. What kind of puzzle can have 500 pieces?
34. What game features Dirk the Daring?
35. Which one of these is not a Rocky figurine?
    a. Mr. T
    b. Apollo Creed
    c. Wally Cleaver
36. What's the most famous blimp in the world?
37. True or false: Wet Banana is the name of a banana-shaped pen.
38. What kind of animal is Garfield?
39. Which one of these is not a speed in rotations per minute at which a record moves on a turntable?
    a. 15
    b. 33⅓
    c. 45
40. What kind of drink does Lipton make?
41. What kind of sticker goes on the bumper of a car?
42. In the Superman plastic model kit, what is Superman breaking?
43. What are the two main types of peanut butter?
44. What do the TV letters ABC stand for?
45. What does Timex make?

    a. Soap

    b. Watches

    c. Cameras

46. 1G-88 is part of what collection?

47. What kind of fuzzy toy is named after President Theodore Roosevelt?

48. What do you send for if you join the Literary Guild?

49. What does Uncle Ben make?

50. What kind of toy is Zod Monster?

TOYS AND PRODUCTS: ANSWERS

1. St. Patrick's day
2. Sixty-four
3. Coleco
4. GI Joe
5. Wendy's
6. Michael Jackson
7. A king
8. Ping-Pong
9. A rabbit
10. Pitfall Harry
11. Frankenberry
12. Candy canes
13. Cracker Jack
14. Cabbage Patch dolls
15. A fortune cookie
16. 2600 and 5200
17. Snap, Crackle, Pop
18. Pong
19. The queen
20. Barbie
21. Baskin & Robbins
22. Powerlords
23. Gumby
24. Jell-O

25. Four
26. Poppin' Fresh
27. Commodore
28. c, Starburst
29. The Care Bears
30. They glow in the dark.
31. Ten cents
32. a, bicycles
33. A jigsaw puzzle
34. Dragon's Lair™
35. c, Wally Cleaver
36. The Goodyear Blimp
37. False. It's the name for a waterslide.
38. A cat
39. a, 15
40. Tea (hot and iced)
41. A bumper sticker
42. A brick wall
43. Smooth (creamy) and chunky
44. American Broadcasting Company
45. b, watches
46. The Star Wars collection
47. The Teddy Bear
48. Books
49. Rice
50. A GoBot

Transportation: All-New Questions

1. What does SST mean?
2. What means of transportation was used by the pioneers?
3. Name the only space shuttle that never flew in space.

4. What kind of train travels on one track?
5. How many wings does a biplane have?
6. What kind of boat do Eskimos use?
7. What did the *Titanic* hit that caused it to sink?
8. What kind of vehicle rides on a cushion of air?
9. What kind of boat is a U-boat?
10. What kind of ship do jets land on?
11. What is the name of a two-wheeled vehicle in which one person pulls another?
12. What kind of train goes underground?
13. Facing forward, which side of a boat is "port"?
14. Name the last car in a freight train.
15. What kind of boat helps other boats into harbor?
16. What is another name for a large personal pleasure boat?
17. What kind of transportation do you "hail"?
18. What is an animal-drawn method of traveling on snow?
19. What did an ancient Greek or Egyptian call "a set of wheels"?
20. What method of getting around did the Spaniards introduce to America?
21. What kind of car is best suited to crossing sand?
22. What is the name of the airplane in which the President of the U.S.A. travels?
23. What nationality of people have boats called "junks"?
24. What is the more common name of the dromedary, a desert-crossing form of transportation?
25. Starting at the top, what is the order of lights on a traffic signal?
26. What do we call someone who drives a car for someone else?
27. What word describes a group of commuters who drive to work together?
28. What kind of boat did Cleopatra take down the Nile?
29. What kind of vehicle is made by Yamaha, Suzuki, and Kawasaki?

30. How did Moses travel as a newborn?
31. What is the oldest form of transportation?
32. What kind of shoes have blades on the bottom?
33. What kind of transportation is nicknamed a "chopper"?
34. How many wheels does a unicycle have?
35. What kind of boat carries people and cars?
36. A parade of cars is called a what?
37. True or false: A stop sign has six sides.
38. What do you use to propel a canoe?
39. What kind of vehicles transport money, gold, and other valuables?
40. What kind of vehicle is a Sherman?
41. What do you call holes in paved roads?
42. Where did vehicles in the Mercury and Gemini series travel?
43. What is the maximum legal speed limit on U.S. highways?
44. Fully loaded, which one of these carries the most people:
    a. 747
    b. 707
    c. 727
45. What kind of vehicle was the *Hindenburg*?
46. What do barnstormers travel in?
47. What kind of transportation is the Metroliner?
48. Which one of these goes underwater?
    a. Bathysphere
    b. Dive bomber
    c. Hydroplane
49. What kind of horse-drawn transportation carried passengers along fixed routes in the West?
50. How many people can ride in a Lionel train?

TRANSPORTATION: ANSWERS

1. Supersonic Transport
2. Covered wagons
3. The *Enterprise*
4. A monorail
5. Two
6. Kayak
7. An iceberg
8. A hovercraft
9. A submarine
10. An aircraft carrier
11. Rickshaw (also jinrikisha)
12. A subway
13. The left
14. The caboose
15. A tugboat
16. A yacht
17. A taxi or cab
18. A dogsled
19. A chariot
20. Riding horseback
21. A dune buggy
22. Air Force One
23. The Chinese
24. A camel
25. Red, yellow, green
26. A chauffeur
27. A carpool
28. A barge
29. The motorcycle
30. In a basket
31. Walking (feet)
32. Ice skates

33. A helicopter
34. One
35. A ferry
36. Motorcade
37. False. It has eight.
38. Paddles
39. Armored cars
40. A tank
41. Potholes
42. In outer space (in earth orbit)
43. 55 mph
44. a, 747
45. An airship (or dirigible or zeppelin)
46. Airplanes
47. A train
48. a, bathysphere
49. A stagecoach
50. None

Sports: All-New Questions

1. What sport has uprights?
2. What is Reggie Jackson's sport?
3. What sport uses a puck?
4. How many innings are there in baseball?
5. What are the small knobs or spokes called on the bottom of an athlete's shoes?
6. How many points is a football field goal?
7. How many players are there on a soccer team?
8. How many baseball players are out in a double play?
9. What sport uses a pigskin?
10. What sport is played on a diamond?

11. What sport uses a shuttlecock?
12. The San Francisco Giants play what sport?
13. What sport uses the term "love"?
14. What sport offers its champions the Stanley Cup?
15. What boxer used to be called Cassius Clay?
16. How many pins are there in bowling?
17. What are the three kinds of medals which can be won at the Olympics?
18. How many holes are there in one game of golf?
19. What's a perfect score in bowling?
20. How many events are there in a decathlon?
21. What is it called when a bowler takes two rolls to knock down all the pins?
22. What basketball player was nicknamed Wilt the Stilt?
23. What sport has a matador?
24. What sport is played at Wimbledon?
25. What is it called when a player drops a football?
26. How many balls walks a baseball player?
27. Basketball is played on a:
    a. rink.
    b. court.
    c. field.
28. What sport do the Boston Bruins play?
29. What event determines the baseball championship?
30. Which one of these is not a Los Angeles team?
    a. Rams
    b. Kings
    c. Expos
31. The Kentucky Derby is an event in what sport?
32. Which one of these is not played in a ring?
    a. Boxing
    b. Wrestling
    c. Ice hockey
33. What do you do when you "punt" a ball?
34. What animal is raced in harness racing?
35. What is a "hat trick" in ice hockey?
36. What sport does Jimmy Connors play?

37. Which one of these sports is not played with a racket?
    a. Tennis
    b. Squash
    c. Lacrosse
38. In which sport can you "spike" a ball over the net?
39. In what sport do you "dribble"?
40. What sport uses a foil?
41. What is raced in the Tour de France?
42. "Downhill" and "Alpine" are terms in what sport?
43. What football team has wings on their helmets?
44. What sport do "hoopsters" play?
45. Football legend Vince Lombardi was a:
    a. coach.
    b. quarterback.
    c. announcer.
46. Which stadium is home to the New York Yankees?
47. What is the first name of baseball great Mr. Berra?
48. Which one of these is not a famous jockey?
    a. Willie Mays
    b. Willie Shoemaker
    c. Steve Cauthen
49. What is the present occupation of former basketball great Bill Bradley?
    a. Basketball coach
    b. Sports reporter
    c. U.S. Senator
50. Which one of these is not a kind of baseball pitch?
    a. Knuckleball
    b. Gutterball
    c. Fastball

SPORTS: ANSWERS

1. Football
2. Baseball
3. Ice hockey
4. Nine
5. Cleats
6. Three
7. Eleven
8. Two
9. Football
10. Baseball
11. Badminton
12. Baseball
13. Tennis
14. Ice hockey
15. Muhammad Ali
16. Ten
17. Gold, silver, bronze
18. Eighteen
19. Three hundred
20. Ten
21. A spare
22. Wilt Chamberlain
23. Bullfighting
24. Tennis
25. A fumble
26. Four
27. b, court
28. Ice hockey
29. The World Series
30. c, Expos
31. Horse racing
32. c, Ice hockey

33. You kick it.
34. A horse
35. Three goals scored by the same person in a single game
36. Tennis
37. c, Lacrosse
38. Volleyball
39. Basketball
40. Fencing
41. Bicycles
42. Skiing
43. The Philadephia Eagles
44. Basketball
45. a, Coach
46. At Yankee Stadium
47. Yogi
48. a, Willie Mays
49. c, U.S. Senator
50. b, Gutterball

Fun Game Books from SIGNET